ed
nd
ng

Web Services, Service-Oriented Architectures, and Cloud Computing

The Savvy Manager's Guide

Second Edition

Douglas K. Barry

with

David Dick

AMSTERDAM • BOSTON • HEIDELBERG • LONDON
NEW YORK • OXFORD PARIS • SAN DIEGO
SAN FRANCISCO • SINGAPORE • SYDNEY • TOKYO

Morgan Kaufmann is an imprint of Elsevier

3 1257 02451 2237

Acquiring Editor: Andrea Dierna
Editorial Project Manager: Benjamin Rearick
Project Manager: Anitha Kittusamy Ramasamy
Cover Designer: Alan Studholme

Morgan Kaufmann is an imprint of Elsevier
225 Wyman Street, Waltham, 02451, USA

Library of Congress Cataloging-in-Publication Data
Application submitted

British Library Cataloguing in Publication Data
A catalogue record for this book is available from the British Library

ISBN: 978-0-12398-357-2

For information on all MK publications
visit our website at *www.mkp.com*

Printed in the United States of America

13 14 15 16 17   10 9 8 7 6 5 4 3 2 1

Contents

Introduction

Douglas K. Barry with David Dick

One of the toughest jobs for managers today is keeping up with the rapid changes in technology. An important change in technology is that the future of software will involve service-oriented architectures (SOAs) with some form of cloud computing. More and more services are available on the Internet. Nearly every day we discover new opportunities to connect these services to create SOAs. These SOAs will require less custom software in organizations, but will likely demand more creativity in the selection and assembly of services. This is a natural evolution of software technology and will be explained in this book.

This book is a guide for the savvy manager who wants to capitalize on the wave of change that is occurring with Web services, SOAs, and, more recently, cloud computing. The changes wrought by these technologies will require both a basic grasp of the technologies and an effective way to deal with how these changes will affect the people who build and use the systems in our organizations. This book covers both issues. Managers at all levels of all organizations must be aware of both the changes that we are now seeing and ways to deal with issues created by those changes.

The intent of this book is to give you an opportunity to consider some ideas and advice that just might make it easier for your organization to realize the potential benefits in Web services, SOAs, and cloud computing. No crystal ball exists to tell us the services that will be available tomorrow. Undoubtedly, there will many innovative services that we cannot envision at this time. For that reason, this book presents a straightforward approach that will help you get your organization ready to take advantage of a SOA—in whatever form it takes.

This is a nontechnical book on a technical subject. It assumes no prior knowledge of the technology. It is written with a high-level view at the beginning of the book. As the book progresses, technical details are introduced and explained. You can stop reading at any point once you have enough understanding for your use.

Business Opportunities Addressed

The technologies and concepts described in this book can:

- Expand your information technology options.
- Make your information technology systems more flexible and responsive.
- Reduce development time.
- Reduce maintenance costs.

This book will explain why these promises can be fulfilled. Read through to the end of Part II to see why the technology discussed will eliminate most technological barriers to integrating systems. Part III discusses why the biggest challenge for managers is handling the people issues related to this change. That part of the book also provides tips on how to make development easier.

Structure of This Book

Part I (Chapters 1–4) begins with a high-level story of how a person on a business trip interacts with a SOA based on Web services and cloud computing. Each of these technologies is then explained in more detail. As Part I progresses, technical details are added to the story in a "peeling of the onion" approach.

Part II (Chapters 5–7) deals with the technical forces driving the adoption of Web services, SOAs, and cloud computing. Change in any organization can be challenging.

This part looks at the forces that help or hinder the technical aspects of change using a technique called *force field analysis*. Force field analysis is applied to various integration techniques related to Web services, SOAs, and cloud computing.

Part III (Chapters 8–10) focuses on the people involved in the change. People worry about the future of their jobs and learning new tools and technologies. An organization must address these issues and concerns to achieve success. This part uses the force field analysis introduced in Part II. Here, the analysis deals with managing the human aspect of the change that occurs with the adoption of a SOA with cloud computing, and provides tips on how to make development easier. Chapter 10 introduces an incremental SOA analysis technique that aims to improve the project selection process in a way that also improves the chance of success for the selected project.

Part IV (Chapters 11–14) shifts to getting started with Web services, SOAs, and cloud computing. Chapter 11 provides three basic experiments that use Web services and then uses the story of the business trip in Part I to address more advanced uses of Web services. It ends with a vision of what Web services might mean for the future. Chapter 12 provides design concepts and considerations along with staffing and change issues to take into account when establishing a SOA. It illustrates how properly designed service interfaces can make it easier for an organization to respond to the chaos of modern business. It ends with a discussion of SOA governance. Chapter 13 discusses a way to evaluate external services and the systems and hardware related to cloud computing that support those services. Chapter 14 summarizes the Web services, SOAs, and cloud computing related to the business trip described in Part I.

Part IV (Chapters 15–16) is a reference section. It lists various semantic vocabularies and provides a quick reference guide for the terminology used in this book.

Overview of Web Services, Service-Oriented Architecture, and Cloud Computing

The first part of this book begins with a story that illustrates how a service-oriented architecture using Web services with cloud computing might be used for planning and taking a business trip in the not-too-distant future. The chapter following the story outlines a high-level explanation of the technology and related standards involved in this trip. That leads to the introduction of Web services and service-oriented architectures in Chapter 3. Chapter 4 ends this part with an overview of cloud computing.

Chapter 1

A Business Trip in the Not-Too-Distant Future

Contents

This is a story of a business trip in the not-too-distant future. It illustrates how a business traveler relies on service-oriented architectures. Those service-oriented architectures use Web services along with cloud computing.

The Business Trip

This is the story of C.R., which is short for Connected Representative. In this story, C.R. is about to take a business trip to Europe. This trip is much like any business trip in that it will involve visiting multiple customers in different cities over three or four days and responding to routine tasks from the office. At one time, C.R. carried a cell phone and a laptop on business trips. Nowadays, C.R. carries just a smartphone. On this trip, C.R. will also wear his regular eyeglasses that are augmented with a

3

The term *Web services* can be confusing. It is often used in different ways. Compounding this confusion is the term *services*, which has a different meaning than *Web services*.

In this book, *Web services* is defined as a means to connect services together. A service is software that performs some computing function and has some type of underlying computer system. Although not required, *cloud computing* may provide that underlying computer system.

The assembly of services—internal and external to an organization—makes up a *service-oriented architecture (SOA)*. This is yet another confusing term, since SOA is a design and development style rather than an actual architecture. Nevertheless, the result of that development is commonly referred to as an architecture.

---

heads-up display, an earpiece, and a camera. The eyeglasses communicate with his smartphone.

To start planning his trip, C. R. uses a smartphone application that is part of his virtual personal assistant (VPA). He asks the VPA to find all customers near each stop in his trip and to rank them based on criteria from his organization's business intelligence (BI)/analytics system. Although there are specific customers he wants to visit, he also wants to make sure he is keeping in touch with as many customers as he can. Using the list provided by the VPA, C. R. identifies the customers he might see and makes minor changes in the ranking of customers for arranging meetings. He adds the dates for when he wants to leave and return. Then he asks the VPA to arrange meetings. The VPA sends the meeting invitations. Some invitations are by email and others use C. R.'s social network account; the VPA determines the best way to contact the customers.

Within a few minutes of sending the meeting invitations, one of C. R.'s customers confirms the invitation and asks if he is available for dinner. C. R. accepts the invitation. The VPA updates the travel itinerary and calendar. The VPA will keep C. R. informed of any changes that might occur throughout the trip.

As the day progresses, C. R. receives additional messages. The VPA uses the messages to update C. R.'s calendar. Within a few hours, the VPA delivers information about his flights, transportation arrangements, and hotel reservations in three cities.

Let's depart from this story here for a moment. There are two components to C. R.'s VPA. One component is on his smartphone, which has already been mentioned. Another component exists in the public cloud. This means C. R. can access his VPA using other devices (e.g., someone else's phone or a desktop) should he desire. It also allows the VPA to help manage his life even if C. R.'s smartphone is turned off or unreachable. Many of the travel arrangements described here are handled by the VPA component in the public cloud.

The VPA takes advantage of application programming interfaces (APIs) that use standard semantic vocabularies (the data and the names to use when describing the data). Airlines, hotel chains, car rental companies, restaurant reservation systems, calendaring systems, and many other services on the Internet have agreed to use standard semantic vocabularies. Recently, C.R.'s organization added similar APIs to the repository it maintains in its virtual private cloud so that employees' VPAs can interact with the repository.

C.R. opens his calendar on his smartphone to check his itinerary. The arrangements are fine and he confirms the plans. At this point, his manager receives an itinerary of C.R.'s trip on her calendar that includes the departure and return trips along with hotels where C.R. will be staying. Her VPA alerts her of the update along with a list of assignments C.R. is supposed to complete in the near term. This list prompts her to send a message reminding C.R. to review several documents in the documentation repository in his organization's virtual private cloud. C.R. will browse these documents sometime during his trip. C.R.'s spouse also receives updates to her personal calendar that include the departure and return trips along with hotels where C.R. will be staying and hotel phone numbers inserted in the appropriate days. This is something she likes to have handy when C.R. is traveling. Her VPA did not alert her of the change since it knows this type of calendar update from C.R. is not something requiring a notification to C.R.'s spouse.

The itinerary created by the VPA includes links to information about the customers to be visited (including addresses). C.R.'s VPA ensures the address information is stored locally on his smartphone. The global positioning system (GPS) on his smartphone uses these addresses while C.R. is driving.

The morning that C.R. is to depart, his smartphone awakens him two hours early (C.R. uses the alarm clock feature of his phone and his VPA knows when he expects to get up). The reason for waking C.R. early is that there is a serious accident with a chemical spill on the direct route C.R. would normally take to the airport. The VPA recognized that C.R. is going to need more time to get to the airport. Once in his car, the VPA suggests an alternate route. This is based on the traffic information provided as a service by the local department of transportation (DOT). The DOT service tries to make the most efficient use of the routes around the airport, given that the chemical spill will take many hours to clean up. To route traffic, the DOT service uses information provided by thousands of VPAs, the clients of which will be traveling to or near the airport. The VPAs and the DOT service negotiate travel routes that the VPAs then suggest as alternate travel routes to their clients (like C.R.).

Thanks to C.R.'s VPA, he arrives at the airport, in time to check in his baggage, pass through security, and eat lunch before boarding his flight.

The first stop on his trip is Bonn, Germany. As C.R.'s plane approaches the gate at the Cologne Bonn Airport, the VPA recognizes it by the geolocation and also determines that this is C. R.'s first visit to this airport. So, the VPA prepares to provide C. R. with help to navigate through the airport. As C. R. departs the plane, the VPA uses the arrival gate information from the airline service and a map of the airport to tell C. R. via his earpiece how to walk to customs. Once through customs, the VPA guides C. R. to baggage and then to a car. On the way, VPA checks C. R. in with his car rental service and C. R.'s phone receives details about where he can pick up his rental car.

At the parking garage, C. R.'s VPA displays the stall number and car license number on the heads-up display of C. R.'s eyeglasses. When leaving the garage, the security guard scans a code on C. R.'s smartphone and his driver's license to confirm authorization to leave with the rental car. C. R. will not have trouble navigating to his appointments because his glasses and smartphone provide a voice-activated personal navigation system with turn-by-turn guidance, voice instructions, and real-time traffic reports. C. R.'s VPA filters the traffic reports so that C. R. only hears what the VPA "knows" he will consider useful. The VPA has chosen a hotel in the heart of Bonn where C. R. will stay the evening, and it is located near a restaurant that the VPA also "knows" C. R. will like.

While driving, C. R.'s VPA reports a significant problem that a customer is having with one of the products from C. R.'s organization. This is good to know before going into his first meeting. C. R. asks his VPA to collect recent information about this customer and the problem with the product. Once C. R. is in his room, the VPA reminds him that the information he requested is now available from both the customer relationship management (CRM) service that resides in the public cloud and the organization's repository in its virtual private cloud. C. R. also calls the representative assigned to the problem to ask for any additional information before tomorrow's meeting.

After a day of visiting customers, C. R. forgets where he parked his car in a large parking ramp. C. R. easily finds the car because the rental company equipped the car with location tracking. C. R.'s VPA accesses the rental car service in the public cloud and provides C. R. with audio and visual instructions to where the car is parked.

From Bonn, C. R. takes an express train to Paris, France. When C. R. arrives at Gare du Nord, he is eager to get to the hotel and rest. This station is a busy metropolitan destination for travelers. Using the online taxi tracking service, the VPA determines that the crush of arrivals means there are no available taxi stands without a long waiting line in the proximity of the train station. The VPA directs C. R. to a nearby Paris Métro stop with guidance to the route to take and where to get off near his hotel. C. R. pays the Métro fare using his smartphone.

At the hotel, C. R. receives a telephone call from a customer inviting him to lunch at a bistro a short walk from the hotel. C. R. phones the customer and confirms that he would be delighted to have lunch and confirms the time. When C. R. gets outside the hotel, his glasses display the directions to the bistro.

C. R. arrives at the bistro a few minutes before the customer. Arriving early allows C. R. to review background information about the customer the VPA provides him from his organization's repository. C. R has never met this customer before, but he is not worried about not recognizing him because his smartphone can match the telephone number with the geolocation of the customer's cell phone. When the customer arrives, the smartphone sends a signal to C. R. and displays a recent photo of the customer from a social networking site on his glasses. C. R. stands up from his chair to greet the customer.

After an aperitif and pleasantries, the waiter brings the menus. The menu is in French and although C. R. cannot read French, his glasses allow him to read the menu in English. He places his finger under an item on the menu and hears the translation in his earpiece just loud enough that only he can hear. The VPA also checks an online allergy service and informs C. R. if there is a chance the menu item might trigger any of C. R.'s food allergies.

After a busy day of visiting customers, C. R. takes the Métro to the Louvre Museum. His VPA provides directions. From past visits to museums, the VPA has learned that C. R. particularly likes works by Impressionist painters and indicates where they can be found in the museum. At the Louvre, his glasses sense when he stops in front of a particular artwork, then his VPA works with a cloud-based service to recognize the artwork and provide commentary on the art. The VPA knows C. R. is particularly interested in the year something was painted, background on the artist, and who influenced the artist's style. The commentary plays quietly in his earpiece at a volume no one else can hear because, based on his geolocation, the VPA "knows" C. R. is in a museum.

The next stop is London, England. From Paris, C. R. takes the Eurostar train under the English Channel to London's St. Pancras Railway Station. In preparation for arrival, the VPA recommends that taking the Underground to the customer's office is faster than a taxi and provides the quickest Underground lines to take and waiting times. The VPA will provide commentary and walking directions out of the Underground and through the streets of London.

C. R. receives a notification from the VPA of a scheduling change and that he should check his calendar. He opens his calendar on his smartphone and sees that the last customer he wanted to see has canceled (a link inserted by the VPA to a corresponding e-mail message explains why, and asks if he is available for a video chat instead) and that two different customers were added to the trip (based on his earlier rankings). These customers are in a city outside of London. This requires changing C. R.'s current hotel reservation, arranging a hotel in the new city, and making train reservations to the city (all arranged by the VPA). The VPA sends notifications to C. R.'s spouse and manager as well.

With the permission of his customers, C. R. records every meeting (sometimes with photos or video using his glasses). After each meeting, C. R. dictates additional

By now, you have probably noticed that C.R's organization has very current and detailed information on every customer contact. The organization found that in its industry, this makes a big difference in how well employees can support their customers. It also identifies any need that customers might have for additional products or services. This customer information is aggregated from multiple sources, both internal and external to C.R.'s organization.

observations and the VPA sends his observations and the recorded meeting to an online service that reduces it to a summary. Later in the trip, C.R. reviews the summary and makes minor changes before submitting it to his organization's repository.

With some customers, C.R. was able to sign contracts. He scanned the contracts with his smartphone. A scanning service converted them to PDFs and added the appropriate identification details for use by his organization's BI/analytics system. The VPA routed the scanned contracts to the CRM service, the repository, and the appropriate people in C.R.'s organization so that they could immediately start working on the agreements.

The next morning, C.R. receives a notification that his flight is canceled. The airline, however, offers him an alternate flight that will leave early the next morning. C.R. confirms the reservations. The VPA arranges a hotel room near the airport and sends a text message to C.R.'s spouse describing the changed plans. C.R. uses this free time to have a video chat with the customer he could not meet earlier in the week.

Throughout the trip, the VPA collected C.R.'s expenses. He used his smartphone to pay for everything except for small cash expenses that C.R. told his VPA to record as he went. The VPA interacted with a service that manages expense reports and used one of the expense report formats approved by C.R.'s organization. When C.R. returned to the office, he reviewed the expenses, made a few minor changes, and submitted it to the expense report service. The service submitted the necessary information to the external payroll processing service used by C.R.'s organization. C.R. will receive his expense reimbursement on his next payroll check.

Summary

A lot of technology is involved behind the scenes of this story. There obviously need to be agreements and standards among organizations to make this level of data interchange possible. This technology and the standards make it possible for C.R. to be "connected" on his business trip. Chapter 2 provides a high-level explanation of the technology and standards that made this possible.

Chapter 2

Information Technology Used for the Business Trip

This chapter provides a high-level explanation for the technology and standards used for the business trip described in Chapter 1. Many services and supporting technologies came together in the business trip story, including documents and customer data from internal systems, an external customer relationship management (CRM) service, calendar services, a travel website, a car rental service, and more.

Keeping Track of Detailed Customer Data

Remember that C.R.'s organization decided it was important to keep a significant amount of data on each of its customers. C.R.'s organization did not always have data in one place. Before the organization decided to develop a service-oriented architecture (SOA), some customer contact information was in its CRM system, some data was in the accounting system, and still more data was scattered in other internal systems and in such places as the representative personal records and trip reports.

C.R.'s organization first tried to consolidate its customer data using an enterprise data warehouse. As part of that process, C.R.'s organization decided it was time to establish some standards that would help it when using Web services. The first standards effort was to research semantic vocabularies and find one it could adopt and augment with vocabulary unique to the organization. The second effort was to decide on the Web services message protocol that it would use with this semantic vocabulary for its internal systems and services. This protocol was used to communicate with the new enterprise data warehouse.

It was not long after establishing the enterprise data warehouse that C.R.'s organization realized that it underestimated the growth of the data and that the forecasted demands on the business intelligence (BI)/analytics systems would outstrip the resources of its data center. So, it chose to work with a virtual private cloud provider that had a database management system that could handle the "big data" C.R.'s organization was generating on its customers. The cloud provider had the flexibility— called *elasticity*—to devote more resources on demand for the peak uses of the BI/analytics services. Also, the tools the cloud provider had made it easy to develop custom smartphone applications that use the application programming interfaces (APIs) needed to access the data and interact with the BI/analytic services. The virtual private cloud provided C.R.'s organization with the level of security that it wanted for its data.

Using Virtual Personal Assistants

Virtual personal assistants (VPAs) are central to this story. C.R's VPA is software and, in our story, it uses artificial intelligence to reason and learn from experience. The wealth of connections available on the Internet makes it possible to create various types of VPAs that can take advantage of those connections.

Semantic vocabularies and Web service messaging protocols are critical to understanding service-oriented architectures. They are explained in Chapter 3.

Cloud providers and cloud computing are discussed in Chapter 4.

Figure 2.1 illustrates that C. R.'s VPA has a component that is a service much like other services in the cloud. C. R.'s smartphone interacts with the VPA component in the cloud. The VPA service in the cloud acts independently.

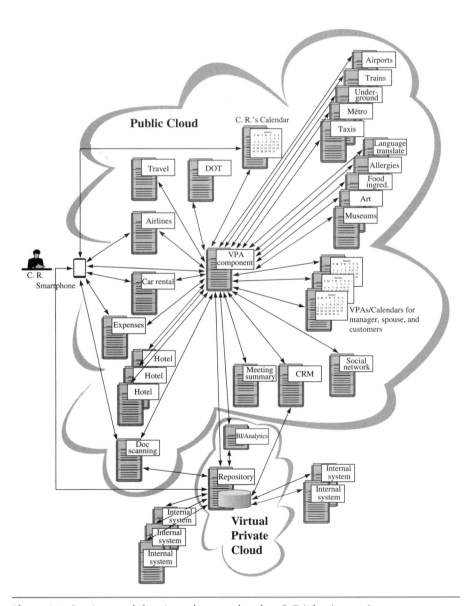

Figure 2.1 Services and data interchange related to C. R.'s business trip.

Managing C. R.'s Business Trip

C.R.'s VPA managed the business trip. It was able to gather information from different services, make travel arrangements, monitor data feeds, "jump" in at the last moment when needed, and provide C.R. with just the information he needed. Thereby, C.R. was able to do what he does best (schmoozing with customers) without overburdening him with having to manage his trip himself or sort through a flood of information.

One illustration of the VPA's role with various services was how it "knew" to monitor traffic information from the local Department of Transportation (DOT) the morning C.R. needed to get to the airport. The accident with a chemical spill that closed a road was also noted by thousands of other VPAs. The DOT service had the capability to negotiate with all those VPAs to come up with a plan to route traffic around the accident. All that C.R. had to do was realize why his wake-up alarm was earlier than expected, and to follow his VPA's suggested detour to the airport that the DOT provided to the VPA.

Augmenting C. R.'s Experiences

C.R.'s VPA also interacted with his eyeglasses that were augmented with a heads-up display, an earpiece, and a camera. His VPA was able to "appear" whenever needed by accessing a myriad of services in the cloud so that it could help C.R. negotiate the city streets, avoid food allergies, translate a menu from French to English, learn more about the art he was viewing, and so on.

Commoditizing Services

Some services are likely to become commodities. Car rental services, for example, will need to agree on certain standards so that they can interact with travel agency and airline services. Those standards could very well mean that it is easy for any consumer (or VPA) to switch car rental services.

In the introductory story in Chapter 1, there are similar standards for cloud-based services for hotels, trains, subways, airports, museums, and so on.

> Of course, for this to happen there needed to be standardization of the types of messages and data exchanged. For the sake of this story, we will assume that the various industry consortia were able to develop those standards.

Viewing All Services the Same Way

Although the semantic vocabulary and message protocol may vary among services, in a sense, they all appear the same. C. R. or his VPA do not need to know if a service is in a public cloud, a virtual private cloud, or supported by an aging internal system in C. R.'s organization. The interaction is similar and there is no need to know where a service is physically located.

Summary

In all likelihood, there are probably many hundreds of services used during C. R.'s business trip. There are also SOAs assembled from the services. C. R.'s organization has an SOA that mixes public and virtual private cloud computing with the non-cloud computing of its internal systems. Many of the services shown may have their own SOA. Among those that might include the airlines, car rental, and local DOT. The VPA component also undoubtedly has a sophisticated SOA. Chapter 3 will explain SOAs and Web services.

Web Services and Service-Oriented Architectures

Contents

Service-oriented architecture is a way to design, implement, and assemble services to support or automate business functions. Various Web services can be used to connect services. This chapter first explains Web services connections. It begins with **15**

More often than not, you can look to the past to find a pattern that will allow you to predict the future. I had an epiphany of this sort concerning the future of software systems architecture back in 2002 when I was writing the first edition of this book. At the time, I was upgrading my AV system. The past for this analogy is my old AV system and the future is the continued evolution of my AV system.

Since 2002, I have continued to evolve my AV system. The cable box was replaced with a digital video recorder (DVR) from my cable company. The VCR was removed, and I decided to resurrect an old turntable to play some of my vinyl albums. I have kept the same receiver and have resisted getting a flat-screen TV. All these components were connected using RCA connectors.

When we recently moved into a new home, my wife and I decided it was time to upgrade to a high-definition TV (HDTV). Of course, I now need to use high-definition multimedia interface (HDMI) connectors, yet I still have my old CD player and turntable. The DVR needed to be upgraded to HD and we purchased a new receiver that could handle HDMI as well as the older audio inputs that use RCA connectors. Figure 3.1 shows how I connected the various components.

an analogy to connections used in audio-video (AV) systems (specifically, services in a service-oriented architecture are to AV components as Web services are to the connections between AV components). The connection technology of Web services is explained along with the importance of standardized semantic vocabularies. Then service-oriented architectures are explained in more detail.

What does this have to do with software systems architecture? Well, it's all in the connections. Web services are connections not unlike those we have with AV systems. Moreover, just like AV systems, we will be able to assemble components in all sorts of ways because of those connections. In much the same way that that RCA and HDMI connectors are used to connect components to carry standardized audio and video signals, Web services connections increasingly use standardized

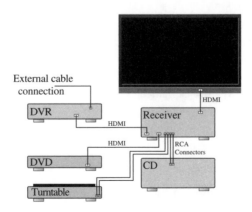

Figure 3.1 AV components.

semantic vocabularies to transport data (I'll explain more about vocabularies later in this chapter).

Service-Oriented Architecture Overview

The business trip that C.R. took in the introductory story in Chapter 1 involved using multiple services, both inside and outside his organization, such as travel, car rental, online calendar, and customer relationship management (CRM) services. From a software architectural point-of-view, this is a *service-oriented architecture* (SOA). An SOA is built using a collection of services that communicate with each other. The communication can involve either simple data passing or it could involve two or more services coordinating some activity. Some means of connecting services to each other is needed. Those connections are Web services. The Application Program Interface (APIs) mentioned in Chapters 1–2 use Web services.

SERVICES

A service is software and hardware. One or more services support or automate a business function. Most often, the intent is that a service can be used in multiple ways (often referred to as *reusability*). There are two types of services: atomic and composite. An *atomic* service is a well-defined, self-contained function that does not depend on the context or state of other services. A *composite* service is an assembly of atomic or other composite services. A service within a composite service may depend on the context or state of another service that is also within the same composite service.

The analogy to AV components fits well here. Manufacturers have decided on the basic functions of a DVD player, a DVR, and other components. Most of the AV components are analogous to composite services. For example, the turntable in our example also has a preamp. Audiophiles might prefer a separate preamp. In that case, both the turntable and the preamp would be analogous to atomic services.

Organizations will eventually evolve standard capabilities of CRM, enterprise resource planning (ERP), and other services. These will become standard services and could, in some ways, be seen as commodities. We may see these services come in various forms, just as AV components do today.[1]

What does this mean for software development? It means fewer people writing software and more organizations buying software or renting access to software rather

---

[1] The organizations working on the various standards can be found at *http://www.service-architecture.com/web-services/articles/organizations.html.*

than building it. Continuing with the AV analogy: I am old enough to have built my share of Heathkit electronic kits for audio and other systems. (This was much like building your own software.) The Heathkit era for electronics is over. I believe a lot of software development will go the same way.

CONNECTIONS

Web services provide the means of connecting services. Just like there are multiple types of connections that can be used in an AV system (RCA, HDMI, etc.), there are multiple types of Web services for connection services (they will be discussed next in the "Web Services Explained" section).

Connections such as Web services are part of the inevitable evolution of interconnectedness. Consider how we can now exchange email among disparate products. Although we could not do that at one time, we now take it for granted. This e-mail exchange is possible because of standards. Connections like Web services (or the equivalent) will also be taken for granted some day because sets of standards will be developed.

Figure 3.2 illustrates a basic service-oriented architecture. It shows a service consumer at the right sending a service request message to a service provider at the left. The service provider returns a response message to the service consumer. The request and subsequent response connections are defined in some way that is understandable to both the service consumer and the service provider.

A service provider can also be a service consumer. In the story of C. R.'s business trip, most of the service providers were also service consumers. For example, the virtual private assistant (VPA) service provided travel information, but to do that it needed to consume information from hotel services, car rental services, calendar services, and more.

THE ARCHITECTURE IN SOA

There is more to the architecture of an SOA than described here. There are issues such as the granularity of services, loose coupling, composability, and more that need to be considered when designing a service-oriented architecture. Concepts related to these issues are described later in this chapter.

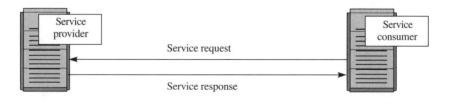

Figure 3.2 SOA basics.

Web Services Explained

Earlier, Web services were described as a connection technology. To get a full understanding of Web services, the history of the first Web services specification is discussed here.

HISTORY OF WEB SERVICES SPECIFICATION

Originally the only Web services specification included the Web Services Description Language (WSDL); Universal Description, Discovery, and Integration (UDDI): and SOAP. Over time, interest in UDDI has faded. Just to give you historical context, here is an overview of how the original specification was intended to work.

Web Services Description Language

WSDL forms the basis for the original Web services specification. Figure 3.3 illustrates the use of WSDL. At the left is a service provider and at the right is a

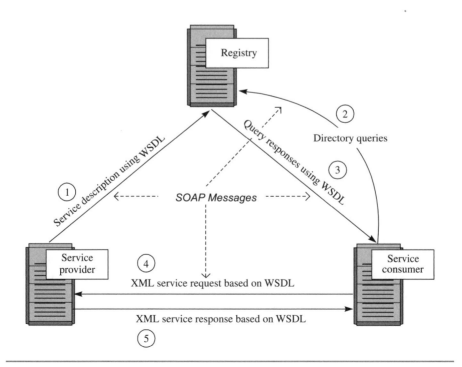

Figure 3.3 Web services basics.

service consumer. The steps involved in providing and consuming a service are as follows:

1. A service provider describes its service using WSDL. This definition is published to a registry of services. The registry uses UDDI.
2. A service consumer issues one or more queries to the registry to locate a service and determine how to communicate with that service.
3. Part of the WSDL provided by the service provider is passed to the service consumer. This tells the service consumer what the requests and responses are for the service provider.
4. The service consumer uses the WSDL to send a request to the service provider.
5. The service provider provides the expected response to the service consumer.

Universal Description, Discovery, and Integration

The UDDI registry was intended to serve as a means of "discovering" Web services described using WSDL. The idea was that the UDDI registry could be searched in various ways to obtain contact information and the services available from various organizations. UDDI registries have not been widely implemented.

The term *registry* is sometimes used interchangeably with the term *service repository*. Generally, repositories contain more information than a strict implementation of a UDDI registry. Today, instead of active discovery, repositories are used mainly at design time and to assist with governance.

SOAP

All the messages shown in Figure 3.3 are sent using SOAP. (SOAP at one time stood for Simple Object Access Protocol; now the letters in the acronym have no particular meaning.[2]) SOAP provides the envelope for sending Web services messages. SOAP generally uses HTTP, but other means of connection may be used. HTTP is the familiar connection we all use for the Internet.

Figure 3.4 provides more detail on the messages sent using Web services. At the left of the figure is a fragment of the WSDL sent to the registry. It shows a CustomerInfoRequest that requires the customer's account to object information. Also shown is the CustomerInfoResponse that provides a series of items on the customer including name, telephone, and address items. At the right of the figure is a

---

[2] Starting with SOAP version 1.2, SOAP is no longer an acronym.

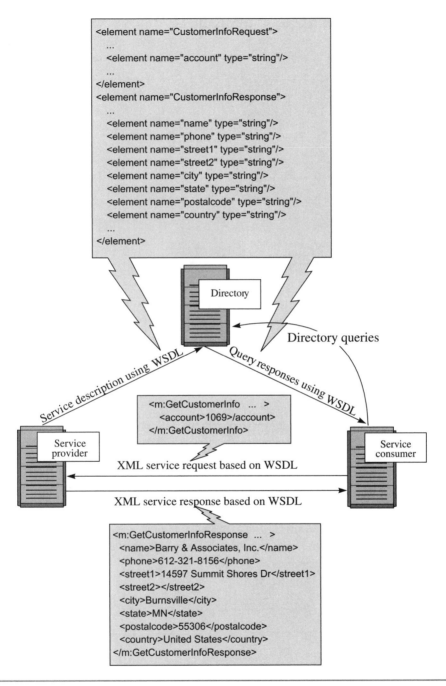

Figure 3.4 SOAP messaging with a directory.

fragment of the WSDL sent to the service consumer. This is the same fragment sent to the directory by the service provider. The service consumer uses this WSDL to create the service request shown above the arrow connecting the service consumer to the service provider. Upon receiving the request, the service provider returns a message using the format described in the original WSDL. That message appears at the bottom of Figure 3.4.

WEB SERVICES SPECIFICATIONS

There are multiple specifications that can be used for Web services. This section shows examples for SOAP/WSDL without UDDI, REST, XML, and JSON.

Using SOAP without UDDI

It is possible to use SOAP without UDDI. The connection is, instead, "hard-coded" if you will. The resulting interaction involves only the bottom part of Figure 3.4. The interaction between the service provider and the service consumer is shown in Figure 3.5. This is the nature of virtually all SOAP Web services today.

Using REST

The first alternative to SOAP that was developed is Representational State Transfer (REST). REST is a style of architecture based on a set of principles that describe how networked resources are defined and addressed. Roy Fielding first described these principles in 2000 as part of his doctoral dissertation.[3]

REST appeals to developers because it has a simpler style that makes it easier to use than SOAP, is a bit less verbose than SOAP (sends less down the "wire"), and is used in a way that other resources are used on the Internet.

Figure 3.6 illustrates a fragment of a REST message. It looks a lot like any other HTTP request that uses parameters. The return message in this example looks much like the return messages from SOAP.

---

[3] Chapter 5 of Roy Thomas Fielding's doctoral dissertation "Architectural Styles and the Design of Network-based Software Architectures" addresses REST. See *www.ics.uci.edu/~fielding/pubs/dissertation/rest_arch_style.htm.*

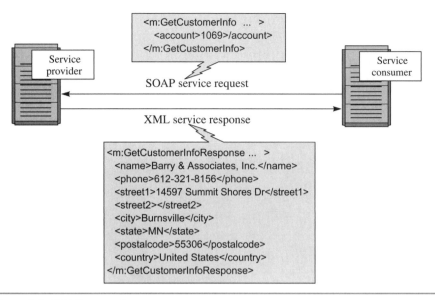

Figure 3.5 SOAP messaging.

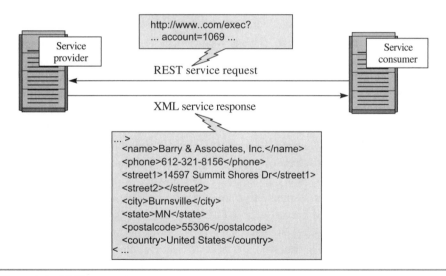

Figure 3.6 REST messaging.

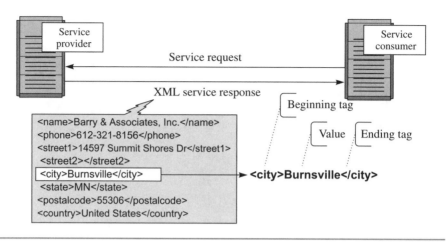

Figure 3.7 Tagged messages.

Using XML

The examples here show both SOAP and REST using XML for response messages. XML has a *tagged* message format. This is shown in Figure 3.7. The tag <city> is highlighted in this figure. The value of city is Burnsville. The tag </city> is the ending tag indicating the end of the value of city. Both the service provider and service consumer use these tags. In fact, the service provider could send the data shown at the bottom of Figure 3.7 in any order. The service consumer uses the tags and not the order of the data to get the data values.

The XML-tagged format provides a level of resilience not available with fixed record formats commonly used before the advent of XML. For example, if a service provider adds an additional element not expected by a service consumer, the XML-tagged format allows processing to continue without any problems occurring.

What if the data sent changes when using XML? Figure 3.8 shows that a service provider has added a new element, <extension> for a telephone extension. The service provider sends a response that includes the new element. As can happen, the service consumer did not know about the new element. Let's see what happens when XML-tagged messages are used.

The service consumer does not expect to receive the telephone extension. Nevertheless, because of the XML-tagged messages, essentially nothing bad happens when extra data (the value of the phone extension) is passed back by the service provider. This is shown at the bottom of Figure 3.9. The tags are used to identify each of the data items and the service consumer uses the proper values. The extra telephone extension data is simply ignored. Although it might be nice to have the extension data, the good news is that no other data is received incorrectly.

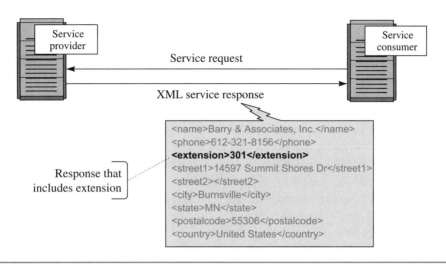

Figure 3.8 Adding a new element.

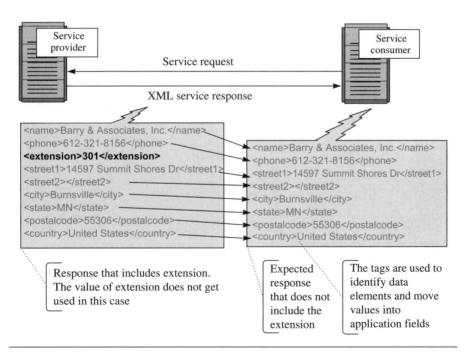

Figure 3.9 Example of the resilience provided by tagged messages.

If a fixed record format was used and the same error occurred, there could be harm. Let's look at this situation. Figure 3.10 shows a fixed record format that passes the same data related to customers. The length of this record is 129 characters. Now, assume the EXTENSION field is added after the PHONE field, but to keep the record length to 129 characters, the STREET2 field is shortened by three characters.

Figure 3.11 shows this change. Assume the same situation occurs as previously described. The service consumer does not know about the new element that contains a value for the telephone extension. Because the fixed record format assumes everything is based on position, whatever appears in a particular position is moved into a field in the service consumer. Figure 3.11 shows that both the EXTENSION and STREET1 fields are moved into the first street address in the service consumer.

Figure 3.12 provides another way to view how this happened. In fixed record messaging, everything is positional. Since the service consumer was unaware of the record change, it moved "30114597 Summit Shores Dr" into the STREET1 field shown at the bottom of Figure 3.12.

The effect of a change like this can vary. Obviously, if the service consumer sent postal mail to this address, it could not be delivered. Less obvious is the situation when a customer record does not have a phone extension. Then the first three spaces of the STREET1 field in the service consumer would be spaces. If the service consumer sent postal mail to this address, it could then be delivered as long as the address was no longer than 22 characters. If the address line exceeded 17 characters then the last part of the address line would appear on the first part of the second address line. That may or may not cause a delivery problem as well. Overall, only some addresses

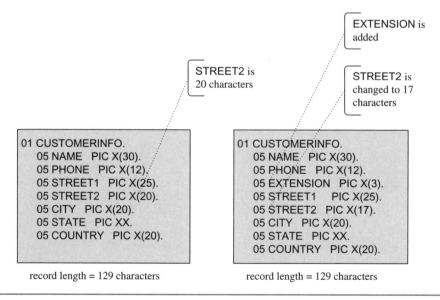

Figure 3.10 Record content changes without changing the length of the record.

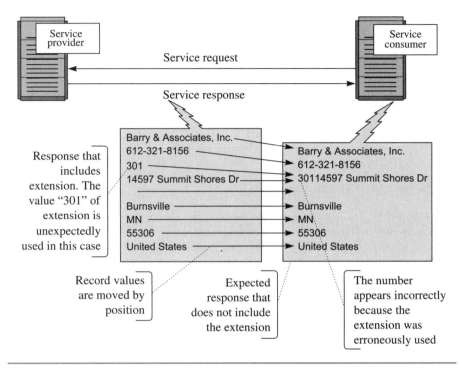

Figure 3.11 Example of the brittleness of fixed record messages.

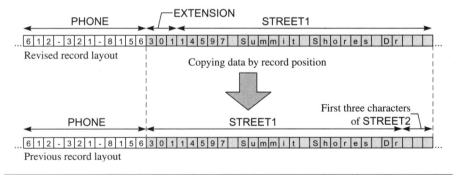

Figure 3.12 How the wrong data can be copied using fixed records.

would fail. Tracking down this type of error is often not easy. Certainly, more catastrophic errors can occur when changing the structure of fixed-length records. There could be situations where the service consumer could even fail because the record layout coming from the service provider is not the layout expected. This issue with fixed records is referred to as *brittleness*.

These types of data format changes occur all the time when exchanging data between systems, either internally or between an internal system and an external system. Using the XML tagged format makes systems more resilient in the face of such changes.

The downside of using XML is that the messages are much longer. XML messages are physically longer than fixed record messages because of the included tag information. So, there is a potential performance hit. With XML, you are trading some resilience in your systems for some reduction in performance. Nevertheless, as transmission speeds increase, this reduction in performance may not be noticed.

JSON, an XML Alternative

It is possible to use Web services without XML. JSON (JavaScript Object Notation) is one option. It uses name/value pairs instead of the tags used by XML. For example, the name "city" is paired with the value "Burnsville." This is illustrated on the right side of Figure 3.13. The name/value pairs in JSON provide the same type of resilience as the XML-tagged format for data exchanges described in the previous section. The name/value pairs do not have to be in any particular order to work.

Figure 3.13 also shows that XML and JSON can use the same vocabulary for the names of the data elements. This opportunity for standardizing on the names and the meaning of the names will be discussed later in this chapter.

When to Use SOAP, REST, JSON, or Other Options

By now, you might be wondering which option is "best" for Web services. If you are using external services, the service providers have chosen the Web service(s) they support. You will need to use whatever they have chosen. In all likelihood, your organization will use "all of the above": SOAP, REST, JSON, and whatever new Web service that is developed. Referring back to the AV analogy used earlier, the type of connections you can use between any two components is limited by the connections they can accept. The choice of Web services is no different.

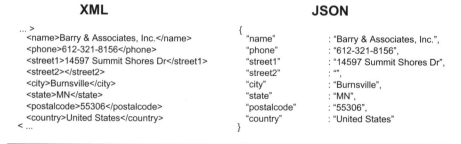

Figure 3.13 Comparison of XML and JSON.

If you are developing your own service, you can choose the Web service that is best for you. The one that is best for you might be the Web service used by most in your industry or the Web service used by most services on the Internet that you are most likely to use. Be prepared, however, to use "all of the above" as mentioned before. However, there may be technical reasons that you should choose one Web service over another. The technical advantages and disadvantages of each type of Web service available are beyond the scope of this book.

THE OPPORTUNITY AND IMPORTANCE OF STANDARDIZED SEMANTIC VOCABULARIES

Within an organization, it is not uncommon to find, for example, that the "account number" in one unit has the same meaning as the "customer ID" in another unit. This is often not documented and, if widespread enough, can lead to added development costs or even processing problems.

If you move to exchanging data among many organizations, the data element name and meanings can vary even more. So, the advent of Web services created an opportunity for industry groups and other organizations to establish standardized semantic vocabularies. This is because the most common means of exchanging data using Web services involves sending the name of a data element along with the value of that data element. This is the example shown earlier, where there is a data element named "city" with a value of "Burnsville." The data exchange includes both the name "city" and its value "Burnsville." XML does this using tags; JSON does it using name/value pairs.

The idea of standardizing on a semantic vocabulary also creates an opportunity for any organization to harmonize data elements among its units and with the larger world outside the organization. If, for example, the meaning of "account number" and many other names is universally understood in a given industry, it can easily minimize development costs and processing errors.

Harmonizing with industry semantic vocabularies is one way to position your organization for whatever might be coming in the future beyond Web services, service-oriented architecture, or cloud computing.

These semantic vocabularies are often referred to as *XML vocabularies*, since XML was used by the first Web services specification. A sampling of these vocabularies can be found on page 179.

Service-Oriented Architecture Explained

SOA is way to design, implement, and assemble services to support or automate business functions. SOA is not a new concept. The first SOA for many people was in the 1990s with the use of Microsoft's DCOM or Object Request Brokers (ORBs) based

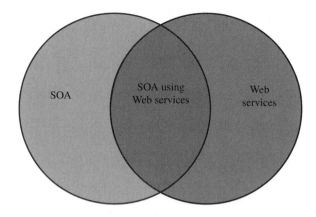

Figure 3.14 Relationship of Web services and SOA.

on the CORBA specification.[4] The basic idea goes back even further to the concept of *information hiding* that creates an interface layer above underlying systems.

RELATIONSHIP OF WEB SERVICES AND SOA

Figure 3.14 uses a Venn diagram to illustrate the relationship between SOA and Web services. The overlapping area in the center represents SOA using Web services for connections. The nonoverlapping area of Web services represents that Web services can be used for connections, but connections alone do not make for an SOA. The non-overlapping area of SOA indicates that an SOA can use Web services as well as connections other than Web services (the original specifications of CORBA and DCOM are examples).

IDENTIFICATION AND DESIGN OF SERVICES

Key to SOA is the identification and design of services. The idea is that services should be designed in such a way that they become components that can be assembled in multiple ways to support or automate business functions. It is not necessarily easy to properly identify and design services. When done well, the services allow an organization to quickly assemble services—or modify the assembly of services—to

---

[4] See page 57 for more on CORBA and DCOM.

add or modify the support or automation of business functions. Here are basic concepts related to services:

■ **Atomic service:** An atomic service is a well-defined, self-contained function that does not depend on the context or state of other services. Generally, an atomic service would be seen as *fine grained* or having a *finer granularity*.

■ **Composite service:** A composite service is an assembly of atomic or other composite services. The ability to assemble services is referred to as *composability*. Composite services are also referred to as *compound services*. Generally, a composite service would be seen as *coarse grained* or having a *larger granularity*.

■ **Loosely coupled:** This is a design concept where the internal workings of one service are not "known" to another service. All that needs to be known is the external behavior of the service. This way, the underlying programming of a service can be modified and, as long as external behavior has not changed, anything that uses that service continues to function as expected. This is similar to the concept of *information hiding* that has been used in computer science for a long time.

The design challenge is to find a balance between fine-grained and coarse-grained services to minimize communication overhead yet keep the services loosely coupled. Chapter 10 provides an approach for designing atomic and composite services.

Service-Oriented Architecture

So, what exactly does a service-oriented architecture look like? Let's start with a service provider. Any given service provider could provide multiple services. Multiple services are represented in Figure 3.15 by the small circles. Services are code—running on an underlying computer system—that provide computing as well as access and updates to stored data.

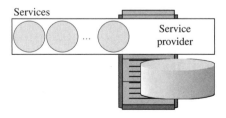

Figure 3.15 Services in a service provider.

Services are assembled to support or automate business functions. Figure 3.16 illustrates the assembly of services. This represents an SOA. Web services are used to connect the services in an SOA.

The services in an SOA can come from any service provider (which, as mentioned earlier, can also be a service consumer). So, in a given SOA, the services might be from internal systems along with any number of external systems accessible anywhere on the Internet. This is illustrated by Figure 3.17.

It is easy to imagine that you can reassemble the same services with other services to achieve a different functionality. This ability to change the assembly of services is one way that an SOA can quickly adapt to changing business needs.

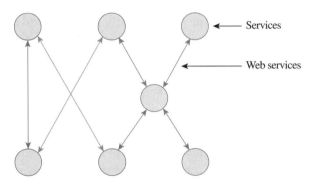

Figure 3.16 Assembly of services into an SOA.

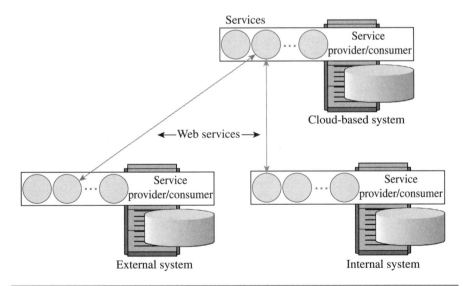

Figure 3.17 Example sources of services in an SOA.

It is also easy to imagine the number of available services quickly expanding to some unmanageable number. That is one reason why governance is important. Governance applies a structure and control over an organization's use of services. Chapter 12 will discuss governance in more detail.

Summary

This chapter outlined Web services and service-oriented architectures. It showed the importance of a robust messaging format in the use of Web services. The chapter also highlighted the importance of the ongoing standardization of the various semantic vocabularies. The chapter ended with an explanation of service-oriented architectures.

Chapter 4 will weave the concepts of service-oriented architecture into a discussion of cloud computing.

Chapter 4

Cloud
Computing

Contents

Chapter 3 discussed services and how Web services are used to connect services. When you place those services in a data center and connect to them over the Internet, you have the basis of cloud computing. The advent of relatively inexpensive hardware (servers and storage) along with the growing availability of high-speed Internet connections made it possible to develop large data centers that can be located most anywhere in the world. There is more, however, to cloud computing, and this chapter provides basic information about it.

This chapter also describes ways that organizations of any size can use a service-oriented architecture (SOA) that takes advantage of cloud computing and why most **35**

Continuing with the audio-video (AV) system analogy from the previous chapter, when I started using a digital camera, I loaded the digital photos onto a PC. At some point I decided to upload photos to a website that manages digital photo albums so that it was easier to share photos. More recently, I've had my older physical photos digitized and I uploaded them to the photo album service as well. My high-definition television (HDTV) is connected to the Internet. This means that I can use my HDTV to view photos managed by the photo album service in the cloud.

I actually have more in the cloud. For instance, I have my calendar, some of my music, and multiple email accounts in the cloud. In the cloud, I only pay for what I use. Moreover, some things are free up to a point (a certain storage amount or a certain level of usage). It is inexpensive to have my digital content in the cloud. It also means I can access that content using my smartphone or most any other device connected to the Internet. Figure 4.1 illustrates the use of the cloud with my AV system.

organizations likely will, as a result, experience a blurring of internal and external services. The chapter finishes with descriptions of the types of clouds and categories of cloud providers.

The AV components (receiver, DVD, etc.) are analogous to services internal to an organization. An organization may, for example, use similar email and calendaring

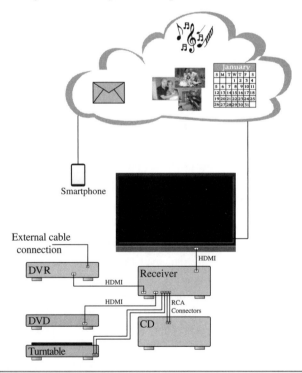

Figure 4.1 HDTV and smartphone connected to the cloud.

services available in the cloud. An organization might also use the cloud for storage, which would be analogous to storing photos or music.

Blurring of Internal and External Services

In an SOA that takes advantage of cloud computing, the distinction between internal and external services will become less apparent. In our story, C. R.'s organization changed from an aging internal customer relationship management (CRM) product to an external CRM service because the external service was more economical and had more functionality. The change may or may not be dramatic, depending on how internal systems were connected to the aging internal CRM product.

Organizations might find that moving more to the cloud greatly simplifies their internal systems—not unlike the AV system analogy. In all likelihood, it is possible to find multiple service providers in the cloud for the same type of service. This creates a dynamic environment, where cloud computing providers compete on features or innovations that are independent of the connections. Competition could be on pricing, content, or other features that allow for highly customized interactions.

Organizations will be affected by additional services becoming available in the cloud. It can be difficult for an internal development group in some organizations to compete with a cloud computing provider that can recoup development costs by having many more customers than any internal development organization could imagine. The external provider can achieve better product at a lower cost because of specialization. Internal development organizations may therefore shift to doing less development. The emphasis internally may shift to making all the connections work properly and integrating new services that might give an organization a competitive edge.

Earlier, I described how I put my digital photos in the cloud and view the photos on my HDTV. Figure 4.1 shows that I kept the turntable and CD player for music that I have owned for a long time. Given my background in software development, I could have digitized my existing music, loaded it on a PC attached to my AV system, and programmed software to manage all that content on my PC. That, however, would be a lot of work and would take a lot of time. I would also need to make sure my infrastructure provides the appropriate backup capability, including off-site backup.

It turned out, however, that I rarely played a CD and never played my old vinyl records. So, I decided it was time to move on. I sold my records and disconnected the turntable and CD player. My HDTV allows for two HDMI inputs. That meant I could also disconnect my receiver. And, I am quite satisfied with using only the online music service. Figure 4.2 shows how much simpler my AV system is now that I am using the cloud for my music.

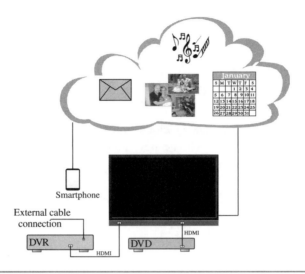

Figure 4.2 Simpler AV system.

It may be obvious what will eventually happen with my AV system. I am using the DVD player less and less to watch movies since most movies I watch now are streamed. My main use of the DVD player is for playing music from the music service in the cloud (the DVD player has an Internet connection). The reason I do this is because to play the music on the HDTV requires the screen to be on, which I don't like. So, once I have an HDTV that allows the screen to be turned off while the sound is left on, I can get rid of the DVD player. Also, my cable provider might provide an alternative to the digital video recorder (DVR) that stores recorded video using a service in the cloud. In fact, the storage capacity of the DVR is limited since I have started recording video in HD. So, I could use some type of elastic storage for my recorded video. With these changes, all I need is a cable box. If a future HDTV allows for cable features such as on demand—or has a place to insert a proprietary cable card—then all I will have in my AV systems is the HDTV. That is simplification.

Organizations of Any Size Can Use a Service-Oriented Architecture with Cloud Computing

The use of an SOA with cloud computing is not limited to large organizations. In fact, this architecture represents an opportunity for small- and medium-size organizations. Many services are provided on some type of fee-for-use basis, which will make them economical for organizations of most any size. Other services are provided at no cost. In the story of C.R.'s business trip, the travel service might charge for each use, whereas the external CRM service might charge a monthly fee for a certain number of users and the car rental and hotel services might be free.

The external expense report service used by C.R. in his trip is an example of a service that can be used by organizations of any size. A one-person organization could either use only the expense reporting portion of the service or download the expense report data into accounting software on a personal computer. A larger organization that uses a payroll service could further automate expense report processing by having the expense report service send reimbursement information to the payroll service.

The Cloud

The cloud provides software and hardware resources via the Internet. The connections into the cloud are often referred to as application programming interfaces (APIs). These APIs use Web services, such as SOAP, REST, and JSON described in Chapter 3. (The cloud component of the virtuaal private assistant (VPA) in the story of C.R. makes extensive use of APIs.) The content sent over these APIs is usually XML or some form of name/value pairs.

Figure 4.3 uses a Venn diagram to illustrate the relationship between Web services, SOA, and cloud computing. Cloud computing is shown within Web services to indicate that cloud computing uses Web services. You can, however, use Web services without cloud computing. As discussed in Chapter 3 with Figure 3.14, you can have an SOA without Web services as well as with Web services. Similarly, you can

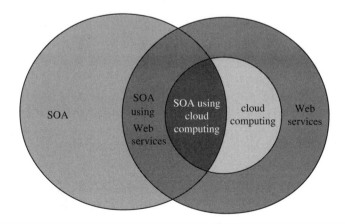

Figure 4.3 Relationship of Web services, SOA, and cloud computing.

use cloud computing without having an SOA. This book emphasizes SOA with cloud computing and using Web services for connections—this is the shaded area of the Venn diagram (SOA with cloud computing).

In Chapter 3, Figure 3.2 illustrated the basics of a service-oriented architecture. That same architecture can be used with cloud computing. Figure 4.4 illustrates a similar SOA, this time with various combinations of cloud computing. A service provider can be in any type of cloud or be an internal service. Similarly, a service consumer can be a service within any type cloud or be an internal service.

The services provided in the cloud come from multiple organizations. These organizations are referred to as *cloud providers*. As a result, the cloud has multiple services provided by multiple cloud providers. A cloud provider

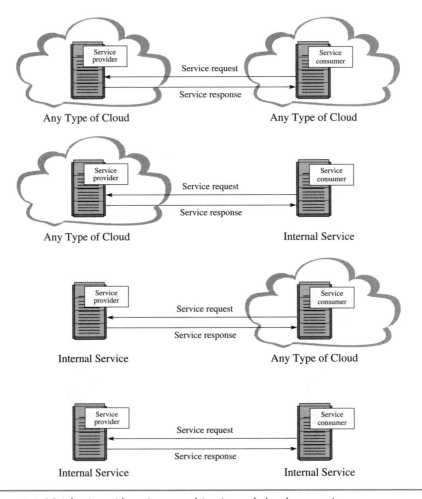

Figure 4.4 SOA basics with various combinations of cloud computing.

usually strives to ensure high-availability of its infrastructure. Some cloud providers have the building blocks to create services: software tools, database management systems, hardware, backup-services, and so on. Other cloud providers have suites of services such as a counting, CRM, document management, and many more. Furthermore, some cloud providers that have suites of services, also provide tools to customize the suites to meet particular business needs.

Cloud providers often price their infrastructure and services on a demand basis. For example, you could pay by transaction or by the amount of storage on-you are using. Some cloud providers have the capability to scale up dynamically for such things as peak transaction loads or unexpected higher storage requirements. The cloud usually allows organizations to avoid significant upfront costs since you only pay for what you use as you use it.

Whether you intend to build your own services in the cloud or use a cloud provider's services, you need to consider issues of security, software tools, and software infrastructure, along with the hardware infrastructure. Security is often a major concern if using a public cloud because it is a shared environment.

Types of Clouds

- **Public cloud:** The email, calendar, photo, and music services used in the AV system analogy are all in the public cloud. Nearly all of the services used by the VPA in the story about C. R.'s trip are also in the public cloud. The VPA itself is in the public cloud as well. Typically, a public cloud provider allows multiple organizations to provide multiple types of services (often referred to as *multitenancy*). The location for the underlying data center could be most anywhere in the world (often referred to as *location independence*). The underlying hardware is usually chosen by the cloud provider and not the users of the service (here you will likely find *virtualization* and *device independence*). The public cloud can also be described as an *external cloud* when viewed from within a given organization.

- **Community cloud:** A community cloud is more restricted than a public cloud. The restriction is to a "community." The restriction could be based on an industry segment, by general interest, or by whatever way a group might be defined. These clouds could be multi-tenanted. The underlying data center might be provided by a third party or by one member of the community.

- **Private cloud:** A private cloud is restricted to one organization. Most often that organization is the single tenant—that is, unless the organization might want to host a private, multi-tenanted cloud for various internal segments or units of the organization. The data center for private clouds is managed by the organization. This can also be called an *internal cloud.*

■ **Virtual private cloud:** C.R.'s organization wanted to get out of the business of maintaining an enterprise data warehouse in its data center and decided to use a virtual private cloud. A virtual private cloud involves some type of partitioning to ensure that the private cloud remains private. Typically, a virtual private cloud provider allows the definition of a network similar to a traditional network. Within such a network, it is possible to have systems such as database managements systems, business information (BI)/analytics systems, application servers, and so on.

■ **Hybrid cloud:** This is the combination of any of the above. In reality, this is a somewhat ambiguous term since an organization might have a private cloud and use the public cloud. That could be seen as a hybrid cloud or it could be simply using two types of clouds.

Categories of Cloud Providers

■ **Infrastructure as a Service (IaaS):** This contains the physical and virtual resources used to build the cloud. These cloud providers provision and manage the physical processing, storage, networking, and hosting environment. This is the data center or, in some cases, the data centers. Pricing is often based on resources used.

■ **Platform as a Service (PaaS):** This provides a complete computing platform. These cloud providers provision and manage cloud infrastructure as well as provide development, deployment, and administration tools. Here you will find the features that make a platform: operating systems, web servers, programming language, database management systems, and so on. This is where the provider might provide elasticity: the ability to scale up or scale down as needed. You will also find some level of reliability provided by the software platform. For example, some type of fault tolerance might be provided for the database management system. In the story of C.R., when his organization wanted to move to a virtual private cloud, it most likely looked for a PaaS cloud provider that provides the software and tools to support existing systems. Pricing can be on many dimensions. For example, pricing could take into account the type of database management system, the level of activity, the amount of storage, and computational time/resources used.

■ **Software as a Service (SaaS):** This provides complete software systems. SaaS is a common way to provide applications such as email, calendars, CRM, social networks, content management, documentation management, and other office productivity applications. SaaS is also known as "on-demand software." (The AV example earlier in the chapter uses multiple SaaS cloud providers—as does the story about C. R.) Pricing is often on per user basis, either monthly or yearly.

Figure 4.5 illustrates the relationship of IaaS, PaaS, and SaaS in the cloud computing stack.

SaaS cloud providers are what most people mean when they refer to "the cloud." They provide the services and related data that can be used directly or combined in some way with other SaaS providers or with your own unique data and services.

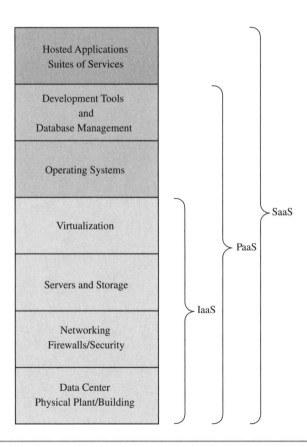

Figure 4.5 Cloud computing stack: IaaS, PaaS, and SaaS.

Summary

The cloud computing model affords the opportunity to deliver applications via the Internet, preclude the costs of owning and operating data centers, and leverage the work of other software developers. This chapter described the categories of cloud providers and, the functions of cloud service management. It also described the relationship among Web services, SOAs, and cloud computing.

The use of any technology, of course, must exist in the context of our organizations. Organizations have many forces that affect the adoption of new technology. The next part of the book will delve into the forces affecting the adoption Web services, service-oriented architectures, and cloud computing.

Technical Forces Driving the Adoption of Web Services, Service-Oriented Architectures, and Cloud Computing

Change in any organization can be challenging. This part looks at the forces that help or hinder the technical aspects of change using a technique called *force field analysis.* Part III will address non-technical, human aspects of change using the same technique.

This part analyzes various integration techniques related to Web services, service-oriented architecture, and cloud computing—with separate chapters on each technology. Each chapter uses multiple force field analyses to build to a concluding analysis on technical forces driving the adoption of the Web services, service-oriented architecture, and cloud computing. Chapter 6, on forces related to service-oriented architectures, builds on the analysis in Chapter 5 for Web services. Similarly Chapter 7, on the technical forces driving the adoption of cloud computing, builds on the analysis in Chapter 6 for service-oriented architectures.

Technical Forces Driving the Adoption of Web Services

Contents

There are two aspects to Web services. One aspect is the vocabulary of the message being sent. The other is the communications protocol that is used to send the message. This chapter will analyze the forces driving both aspects by looking at two representational examples of what was used before the advent of Web services. The examples in this part show that advances in technology and standards have diminished the number of restraining forces, making change more likely to occur.

This chapter introduces force field analysis and applies it to the adoption of Web services. Force field analysis will also be used in the next two chapters on service-oriented architecture and cloud computing.

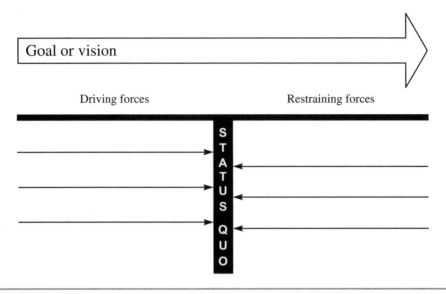

Figure 5.1 Force field analysis.

Force Field Analysis Overview

Force field analysis is a tool that provides a perspective on the forces at work when trying to make changes in organizations. This approach to analyzing change was developed by Kurt Lewin.[1] Figure 5.1 illustrates the concepts of this technique. For any particular activity, there is a goal or vision, which is shown by the large arrow at the top of the figure pointing to the right. There are driving and restraining forces that will impact whether this goal or vision can be achieved.

- Driving forces, which help achieve the goal or vision, are shown as arrows pointing to the right in the same direction as the large arrow at the top.
- Restraining forces, which hinder goal achievement, are the arrows pointing to the left in the opposite direction from the large arrow at the top.

At some point, driving and restraining forces are in equilibrium. This is illustrated in Figure 5.1 by the wide vertical line labeled "Status Quo." Driving forces move an organization from the status quo in the direction of the organization's goal or vision. Restraining forces hold back this change from the status quo. These forces can be external or internal to an organization, or external or internal to the individuals in the organization. The relative strength of the driving or restraining forces determines whether change occurs.

---

[1] Kurt Lewin, *Field Theory in Social Science* (New York: Harper and Row, 1951).

Assume, for example, that you want to change a part of a system in an organization. Two organizational driving forces could be a reduction in operating costs and the opportunity to electronically exchange purchase orders and invoices with a particular customer or supplier. An organizational restraining force could be the development cost for making the change. Figure 5.2 illustrates this concept.

Of course, there could be many other forces at work than those shown in Figure 5.2. The nature of the driving and restraining forces could also vary by organization even if the organizations were attempting to carry out exactly the same tasks. In fact, they can vary among departments in the same organization.

Essentially, the purpose of this model is to make all the driving and restraining forces visible so that decisions concerning change can be made with the best available information. There are various ways to use this model. If you want to make change more likely, you need to either strengthen the driving forces or weaken the restraining forces. Weakening the restraining forces is sometimes the best approach. Strengthening the driving forces can make the restraining forces stronger. In Figure 5.2, developing the electronic exchange capabilities of this change is restrained by the costs of development, effectively resisting change from the status quo. So, perhaps it is possible to adopt an industry standard for electronic exchanges, thus weakening this restraining force. In the figures that follow, weakened restraining forces are shown as gray arrows to indicate that the restraining force is fading away. Figure 5.2, for example, shows the costs of development as weakened and less of a concern.

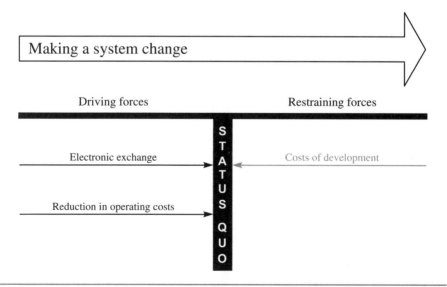

Figure 5.2 Force field analysis for making a system change.

Adopting Standard Data Element Definitions

In the early 1980s, many large organizations were running custom software and there was very little use of packaged software. At the time, it was believed that there would be opportunities to internally exchange data more easily, reduce development time, and possibly reduce maintenance costs if all the custom software were to use the same data element definitions. These opportunities are shown as driving forces in Figure 5.3. Restraining forces related to cost offset these driving forces. Figure 5.3 shows the restraining forces of costs to developing the standard definitions and the costs related to changing existing systems.

There are additional restraining forces in this figure. In some cases, there were valid reasons that two different systems used different definitions for the same data element. At the time, there had been little progress in developing a standard set of data element definitions that could be shared by various organizations. Therefore, the cost of developing a standard set for a single organization was quite high because it involved starting with a clean sheet of paper. Even if efforts to use standard data element definitions had been successful, the first merger or acquisition would likely cause a problem. The systems used by every other organization would likely have

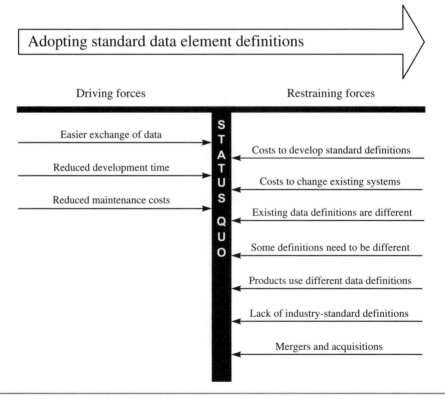

Figure 5.3 Force field analysis for adopting standard data element definitions.

different data element definitions. Finally, as the use of packaged software increased, the definitions used in those products would most likely be incompatible. With enough mergers or acquisitions and use of packaged software, you would be back at the starting point with incompatible data element definitions.

Times have changed since the early 1980s and so have attitudes toward standard data element definitions. Some industries can see advantages in having standard definitions so that data can easily be interchanged among organizations. Another advantage to standard data element definitions is that they lessen the integration efforts involved in mergers and acquisitions. The term *data element definition* has more or less been replaced by *semantic vocabulary*. Chapter 3 discussed the opportunity and importance of standardized semantic vocabularies. A sampling of such vocabularies by industry can be found on page 179.

Adopting a Standard Communications Protocol

There has always been interest in connecting two or more software systems together. This is achieved using a communications protocol. Prior to the introduction of TCP/IP in the 1980s, adopting a communications protocol was a major undertaking.

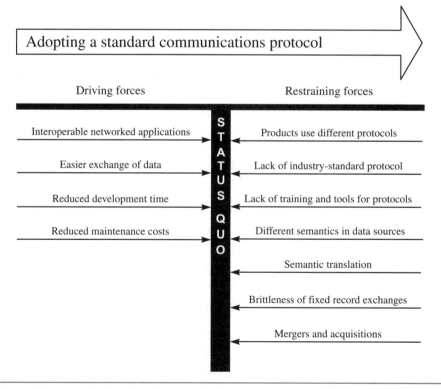

Figure 5.4 Force field analysis for adopting a standard communications protocol.

The intent was that adopting an organizational standard communications protocol should reduce development time and maintenance costs. These are shown as driving forces in Figure 5.4. Before TCP/IP, there was no standard protocol and different protocols could be found among software products offered by various vendors. There was limited training and tools for the protocols since they were often only available from the software vendor or a few third parties. There were most likely differing semantics in data sources requiring semantic translation. The message transmitted was more often than not in a fixed-record format. See page 27 for possible issues related fixed record exchanges. Finally, mergers and acquisitions could easily bring in different communications protocols since there was no standard. Figure 5.4 shows these restraining forces.

Adopting Web Services

Compared to standard data element definitions developed separately for each organization and differing "standard" communications protocols, the use of Web services makes creating interoperable systems much easier. Web services use both XML or name/value pairs for message formats and HTTP with TCP/IP on the Internet for a communications protocol. This greatly reduces restraining forces that had existed prior to Web services. Figure 5.5 shows the driving and restraining forces for adopting Web services.

Figure 5.5 retains all of the driving forces from the prior techniques: easier exchange of data, interoperable networked applications, reduced development time, and reduced maintenance cost. There are also additional driving forces. Many industries are working on industry-wide semantic vocabularies for tagged languages such as XML or other languages that use name/value pairs. This relates to the reduced brittleness driving force. The widespread adoption of Web services has pushed many vendors to incorporate the use of Web services into their products and services. The growing use of Web services also results in a significant growth of external services that can be used by organizations of any size. Similarly, there is an abundance of training and tools on Web services.

The restraining forces affecting the adoption of Web service are fewer and weaker than the preceding techniques. Among the remaining restraining forces are lingering different semantics in data sources and semantic translation. There are, however, efforts in various standards organizations to simplify the semantics and standardize the semantic translation.[2] Those standards are still evolving, which is why they are

---

[2] See *http://www.service-architecture.com/web-services/articles/organizations.html.*

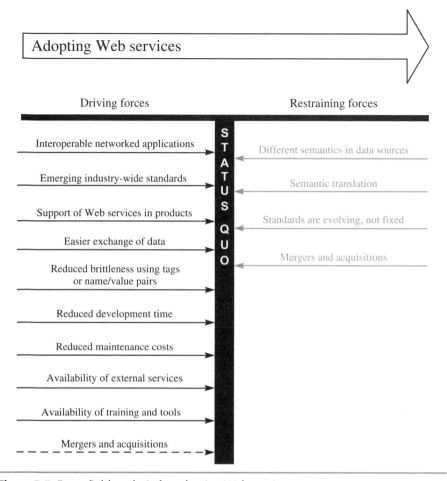

Figure 5.5 Force field analysis for adopting Web services.

seen as a restraining force. Nevertheless, as time goes on these restraining forces will weaken. These weakening forces are shown in gray in Figure 5.5.

Finally, mergers and acquisitions are shown in Figure 5.5 as a weakening restraining force for the adoption of Web services. The broad adoption of Web services by product vendors over time increases the likelihood that an acquired organization will use Web services. Mergers and acquisitions also appear as a driving force. This is for those industries where mergers and acquisitions are commonplace. Easing technical aspects of mergers and acquisitions could, for example, be a driving force for current efforts to develop industry-wide vocabularies for Web services. The reason for the dashed line in Figure 5.5 is because this driving force is not likely to apply to all industries.

Summary

This chapter analyzed the forces driving the adoption of standard vocabularies and communication protocols. It started out by looking at two representational examples of what was used before the advent of Web services. The examples showed that advances in standardized semantic vocabularies and Web services communication protocols have diminished the number of restraining forces, making change more likely to occur.

Chapter 6

Technical Forces Driving the Adoption of SOA

Contents

This chapter applies force field analysis to service-oriented architectures (SOAs). It starts with analyses of integration techniques that preceded SOAs. It then applies force field analysis to the enterprise service bus (ESB), which is often used in SOAs. Toward the end of the chapter, the analyses are combined into a force field analysis of SOAs using Web services. This analysis shows many driving forces for adopting an SOA. It also shows that, over time, many technical restraining forces will diminish and the remaining restraining forces will be typical business and design issues.

Adopting Standard, Enterprise-Wide Software

One early integration technique was for an organization to adopt enterprise-wide software. This worked sometimes. When it did, however, usually it was successful only for a short period. The obvious appeal of adopting standard software is that everyone uses the same software. This means that the entire organization uses the same data definitions, semantics, and formats for exchanging data. Often, this worked best for organizations that were small and were putting a new set of systems in place. Nevertheless, standardizing on systems software often runs into problems, too. There are long-term restraining forces, such as mergers and acquisitions, that can come into play. Even a new, small organization can acquire another organization that uses an entirely different system, and integration problems begin. Figure 6.1 provides the force field analysis for adopting standard, enterprise-wide software.

This approach has a mergers and acquisitions restraining force for a similar reason as seen in trying to establish standard data element definitions in Chapter 5.

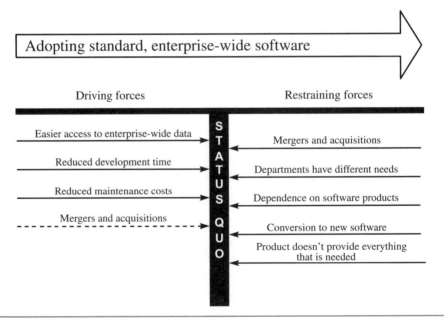

Figure 6.1 Force field analysis for adopting standard, enterprise-wide software.

The other organization can easily use different software. It is also common in larger organizations that some departments have different software needs. It is rare that you can find "one size fits all" software. Another downside is that adopting a complete set of software systems from a single vendor makes your organization dependent on that single vendor. As soon as you move away from that vendor's products, you might be back into common integration issues. For organizations that have existing systems, adopting standard software can mean a mass conversion to the new software. This is often problematic and should be seen as a restraining force. Finally, it is often the case that the product doesn't provide all the functionality that is needed.

Note that none of the restraining forces in this figure are shown in gray. This means that they will not diminish over time and will remain restraining forces for the foreseeable future.

Of course, every example has a counterexample. There are some industries where mergers and acquisitions are commonplace. You will see organizations in those industries adopting common, industry-wide software packages so that it will be easier for one organization to be acquired or merged with another organization. So, mergers and acquisitions can also be a driving force. This is represented in Figure 6.1 with a dashed line. Although I have not seen any empirical data on it, my experience is that this is the exception rather than the rule. That is the reason for the dashed line, because it is likely to apply to only some industries.

Adopting an Object Request Broker

The 1990s saw the introduction of object request brokers (ORBs). The two best known ORBs were the Object Management Group's Common Object Request Broker Architecture (CORBA) specification and Microsoft's Distributed Common Object Model (DCOM). (CORBA is still around in various forms. DCOM is now a part of Microsoft's .NET.)

ORBs are middleware that are one way to exchange data among two or more systems. These systems could be from multiple vendors. In fact, an ORB could be one way to integrate systems from two organizations when a merger or acquisition occurred. An ORB hides the complexity of the communication between two or more systems. They provide a means for applications to communicate with each other. Figure 6.2 shows that, historically, providing interoperable, networked applications was a driving force for adopting an ORB.

The original specifications for CORBA and DCOM, however, dealt with how to get data from one place to another. There were no specific requirements for the

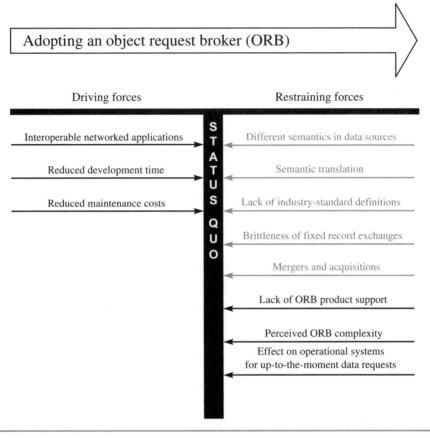

Figure 6.2 Force field analysis for adopting an ORB.

format of the data transmitted in the messages. The restraining forces related to data for an ORB are:

- Different semantics in data sources
- Semantic translation
- Lack of industry-standard definitions

Advances in industry standards such as XML mitigated all these restraining forces, which is why they are shown as gray arrows in Figure 6.2. In fact, using XML makes for a more flexible system because of the tagged record structure of XML.[1] This also mitigated the restraining force related to the brittleness of fixed record formats.

[1] For an explanation of the tagged record structure of XML and the brittleness of fixed record formats, see page 27.

The mergers and acquisitions restraining force diminishes since an ORB would be one way to deal with the multiple systems resulting from a merger or acquisition.

There was a perception in the industry that neither CORBA nor DCOM were widely adopted and that using one or the other or both was too complex for many programmers. Whether the perceived lack of industry adoption or inherent complexity was actually true is irrelevant at this point. These perceptions are seen as restraining forces. Web services have just the opposite perception—they are seen as easy to adopt widely by industry and easy for most programmers to use. Perception in this case might well be the reality.

The very nature of creating interoperable, networked resources means that there could be a negative impact on operational systems when requests come in through an ORB. Many operational systems have not been designed to receive indeterminate or unexpected processing requests. These requests sometimes can have a negative impact on the performance of those systems. So, the effect on operations systems can be a restraining force if up-to-the-moment processing of those requests is needed.

Adopting an Enterprise Data Warehouse

The story about C.R.'s business trip mentioned that his organization had, at one time, an enterprise data warehouse (EDW). An EDW is one of the oldest and most successful ways to integrate and consolidate data from multiple systems. Commonly, it involves extracting data from existing systems and loading it into a single, central location to form an EDW. Using an EDW can be complementary to using an ORB or Web services. The force field analysis for this approach is shown in Figure 6.3.

In this figure, the easier exchange of data as a driving force is replaced with easier access to enterprise-wide data. This data is loaded from existing systems using various techniques that extract, transform, and load (ETL) the data in the EDW. Using ETL techniques means there is usually less impact on operational systems because the extracts of data from these systems could be done at a time convenient for the operational system. This minimal impact on operational systems is a significant driving force. Easier access to enterprise-wide data also allows the use of business intelligence (BI)/analytics software to find patterns or new business opportunities based on a wealth of data that could be stored in an EDW.

Most of the restraining forces are issues with the semantics or meaning of the data and the standardization of data definitions. Not surprisingly, these issues are similar to those involved with attempts at adopting standard data elements when existing data definitions are different. In Figure 6.3, the semantic translation is added to show

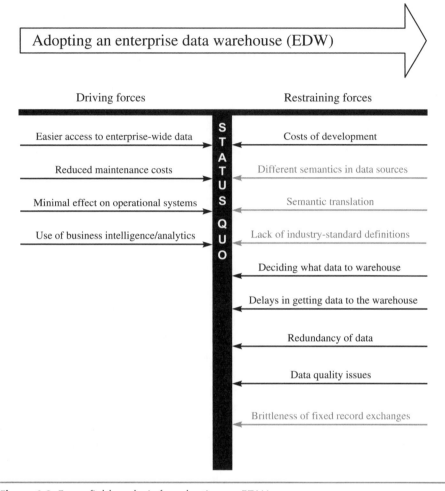

Figure 6.3 Force field analysis for adopting an EDW.

the need to transform data, which can itself be a restraining force. Over time, however, these restraining forces have become weaker for two reasons:

- **A subset of the software industry is devoted to the development of ETL software.** This software generally simplifies the development of the data extractions from existing systems, any semantic translation or transformation, and the loading of the data into the EDW.
- **More industry standards have become available.** Initially efforts were related to electronic data interchange (EDI) and more recently to Web services.

Additional restraining forces include problems related to what data to store in the EDW and the delay or latency in getting data into the EDW. The issue of what data should be stored in an EDW will likely always remain a restraining force. The strength of this restraining force will vary by organization. The delay or latency of data is the result of performing data extracts at times convenient to the operational systems.[2] Consequently, the very latest data is not always available in the EDW. To some organizations, this is no problem. Others, however, may find this a significant restraining force.

Redundancy of data also can be seen as a restraining force. Whenever data exists in more than one location, it is possible that the data will have different values for various reasons. This could result, in part, from the latency of data mentioned earlier. For example, the value of an account balance may be updated by the operational system but not forwarded to the EDW until some later date. At a given point in time, you could see two different values for the same account when looking at the EDW and the operational system.

Data quality issues are potentially a restraining force, because much depends on the quality of the data available. If data to be stored in the EDW is lacking in quality, there are options available for improving its quality. Changes could be made to improve data quality at the time it is entered. For existing data, the quality could be improved at the source. If that is not possible, the ETL software used to load data could be used to improve the quality of the data. Sometimes this is called *data cleansing*. This, of course, assumes the quality can be improved in some way that lends itself to programming. Data quality is a significant topic and you are encouraged to study it further if this is potentially a restraining force for your organization.

Finally, the brittleness of fixed record exchanges is a maintenance issue. If the EDW is changed in some way, it could create a need to change some or all the ETL programs. Because of the nature of fixed record exchanges, there is always a chance that not all ETL programs would be updated and the wrong data would be extracted. As a result, the transform and load portion could fail or the wrong portion of the record could be inappropriately transformed and loaded into the EDW, resulting in essentially a corrupted EDW. This brittleness problem is being addressed by the tagged record structure of XML or name/value pairs (see page 27). The tagged structure significantly reduces the chance of corrupting the data in the EDW and also presents the opportunity to reduce maintenance costs related to ETL programs. So, as a restraining force, the brittleness of fixed records will be reduced. Many of the restraining forces will be reduced because of efforts related to industry-standard semantic vocabularies and Web services as represented by the gray arrows in Figure 6.3.

---

[2] For some organizations, this can be a certain time of day. For others who cannot stop their operational systems, it may be necessary to provide small data extracts throughout the day.

Adopting an Enterprise Service Bus

Often when integrating systems, there is also a need to propagate data among internal systems. For example, if a customer's address is changed in one internal system, you would want that change to appear as soon as possible in other internal systems.

Propagating data changes, however, can lead to complexity because of the possible number of connections among internal systems. If each internal system were directly connected to the other internal systems shown at the bottom in Figure 2.1, you could have up to 10 possible connections. Of course, if you need to propagate an update, such as a customer address, to multiple systems, you could end up in the situation shown in Figure 6.4. In this situation, every system potentially may need to communicate with every other internal system.

MESSAGE ROUTERS

A good solution to this problem is to add a message router to internal systems, as shown in Figure 6.5. Such routers have been around for some time. They are also known as *application routers*. There are various ways a router could know the other internal systems that need to receive a certain type of update. The individual internal systems would not need to know who receives such updates. As a result, the number of interconnections is reduced, as shown in Figure 6.5.

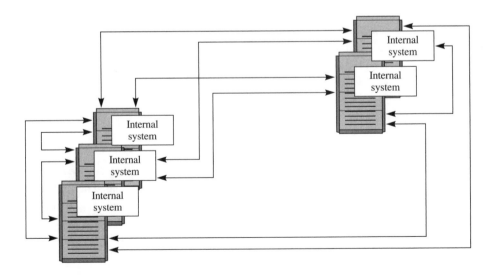

Figure 6.4 Possible connections for internal systems.

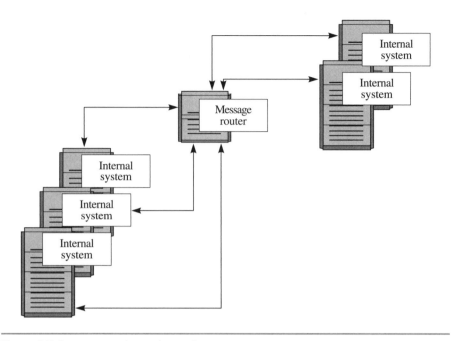

Figure 6.5 Interconnections when using a message router.

A message router usually needs to transform the data in some way to match the format of the data expected by the receiving system. Figure 6.6 shows examples of such transformations. Internal system A at the left is sending data in tagged XML format. Internal system B at the right expects a tagged XML format but expects the tags to be different. For example, instead of the tag <name> in system A, system B expects the data to be tagged with <customer>. The tags for phone and postal code data also are different. Finally, system C expects a fixed record format. This fixed format is shown at the bottom in Figure 6.6.

ADAPTERS

These transformations do not occur automatically. Some type of adapter is needed to transform the data in the messages. Adapters also need to transform instructions that may be needed for communication. Some example instructions are starting a transaction, ending a transaction, getting query results, and so on.

The use of Web services and the development of SOAs created a need for a router that worked with Web services and that had adapters for various existing systems. Those capabilities are provided by an ESB. The term *bus* reflects the analogy of a

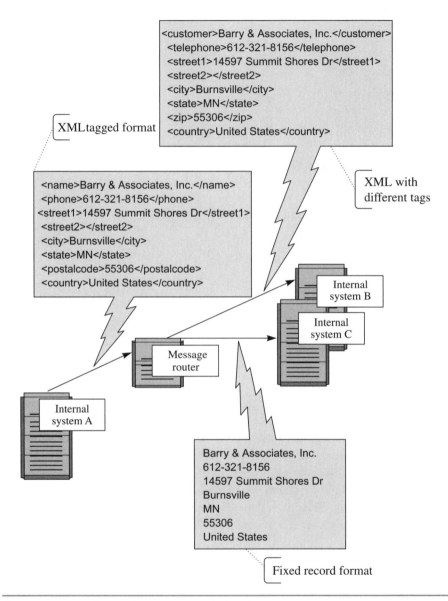

Figure 6.6 Example transformations needed with a message router.

computer hardware bus—a common architecture in computer design that uses standard connections. A computer bus makes it easier to transfer data and instructions among a computer's subsystems. Similarly, an ESB makes it easier to transfer data and instructions among various software systems: services, business processes, applications, legacy systems, BI/analytics software, and so on.

Going back to the analogy of the audio-video (AV) system, the receiver plays a role that is similar to an ESB. For instance, you can assemble an AV system without a receiver just as you can use Web services without an ESB. Nevertheless, a receiver gives you more options and usually facilitates having multiple components—especially if differing ages of the components require different connections (like adapters that connect existing software systems).

An ESB can play multiple roles. As a router, an ESB monitors, logs, and controls routing of messages among services and systems. An ESB's adapters enable the transformation and conversion of protocols and messages. The adapters ensure that the message vocabulary used within the ESB is the organization's standard semantic vocabulary. The delegation of routing, protocol conversion, and message transformation to an ESB gives services and other software systems a convenient way to easily plug into a bus system.

There is no standard feature list for an ESB. If you are considering an ESB, be sure that it provides all the features you need. Figure 6.7 depicts an ESB with adapters for existing software systems.

The force field analysis for adopting an ESB is shown in Figure 6.8. In this figure, a driving force is consistent enterprise-wide data in all applications. This means that

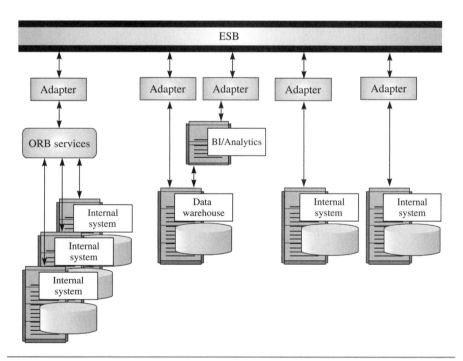

Figure 6.7 ESB with adapters for existing software systems.

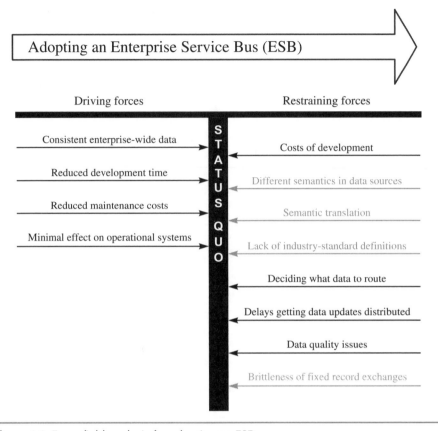

Figure 6.8 Force field analysis for adopting an ESB.

customer data, for example, would be the same no matter what system used or managed that data. The impact on operational systems is minimized since any one system only needs to communicate with the message router and not all the other internal systems.

Most of the restraining forces are the issues with the semantics or meaning of the data and the standardization of data definitions that have been discussed earlier. Message routing, like EDW, needs to deal with semantic translation and this is shown as a restraining force. Over time, however, these restraining forces have become weaker as more industry standards become available.

Additional restraining forces include problems related to what data to route and the delay or latency in getting data updates distributed to various internal systems. The issues of what data to route and the delay of getting data updates distributed will likely always remain restraining forces. Data quality issues similar to EDW can occur with message routing. Obviously, it can be potentially disastrous to route poor-quality data. With message routing, however, you do not have the option of data cleansing used in conjunction with ETL software. The quality of data needs to be improved at the source for existing data and at the point of entry for new data.

Finally, the brittleness of fixed record exchanges is a maintenance issue.[3] If the format of the record going to the message router is changed, it could create a problem. Because of the nature of fixed record exchanges, there is always a chance that the wrong data is routed. This brittleness problem is addressed by the tagged record structure of XML or name/value pairs. Such a structure significantly reduces the possibility of corrupting data routed by the ESB and presents an opportunity to reduce maintenance costs related to message routing programs. So, as a restraining force, the brittleness of fixed records will be reduced over time.

Web services adapters for packaged software provided by vendors also reduce costs of development. The adapters allow Web services connections with internally developed systems or packaged software. The arrow depicting the restraining force of development cost, however, is not shown as gray since there still can be other significant development costs related to an ESB.

An ESB can work with EDWs and existing middleware solutions such as an ORB. This is shown in Figure 6.7. The ESB would have adapters that, in turn, would connect to the EDW and ORB. Note that the ORB is represented as a bus much like an ESB and that it is labeled as "ORB services." This is because an ORB provides communication for services much like an ESB.

Adopting a Service-Oriented Architecture

Web services, middleware integration (i.e. ORB services), data warehousing, and an ESB can all work together to support a service-oriented architecture. Figure 6.7 shows these technologies. This is essentially a more detailed diagram of C.R.'s organization, which was described in Chapter 2. In the bottom of Figure 2.1, you can see the internal systems in C.R.'s organization along with the repository. The three internal systems at the left in Figure 2.1 relate to the three systems at the left in Figure 6.7; this time we add the detail of middleware ORB services with an adapter for these internal systems. The two internal systems at the right in Figure 2.1 relate to the two systems at the right in Figure 6.7. The online repository at the bottom center in Figure 2.1 is shown as a data warehouse in Figure 6.7. Finally, the BI system shown connected to the repository in Figure 2.1 is also shown as connected to the data warehouse in Figure 6.7. The data warehouse, however, is not in a virtual private

---

[3] For an explanation of the brittleness of fixed formats, see page 27.

cloud as shown in Figure 2.1. The reasons C. R.'s organization made that change will be covered later.

The drive to use Web services is reducing the technical change issues. This makes moving to an SOA technically easier. Figure 6.9 shows how using Web services affects adoption of an SOA overall. This figure combines the force field analyses for Web services (see Figure 5.5), enterprise-wide software (see Figure 6.1), ORB middleware (see Figure 6.2), data warehousing (see Figure 6.3), and an ESB (see Figure 6.8). The combined technical restraining forces are shown at the right. The gray arrows represent the technical restraining issues that will diminish as industry adopts and expands the use of Web services.

Three restraining forces from enterprise-wide software (see Figure 6.1) were not added to Figure 6.9: departments have different needs, dependence on software products, and conversion to new software. These represent issues for moving to standard enterprise-wide software. Since an SOA does not require changing to enterprise-wide software, these restraining forces were dropped.

There is an addition to Figure 6.9 related to services. A restraining force has been added at the bottom right in Figure 6.9 for the identification and design of services. This is critical for an SOA and was discussed in Chapter 3 on page 30.

The analysis in Figure 6.9 is interesting because it illustrates that as the technical restraining forces shown in gray diminish, we are left with technical issues related to business and general design. The arrows at the top right represent business issues such as costs of development or concerns that a product doesn't have all the features that might be needed. There are, of course, other design issues, but these arrows are representative of basic design issues facing any effort to create an SOA.

At the left in Figure 6.9 are the driving forces for adopting an SOA using Web services. The strength of these forces will vary by organization. Also, there very well might be additional driving forces for a particular organization. Nevertheless, by almost any measure, there are tremendous driving forces for the adoption of an SOA. You may want to try adding technical driving and restraining forces to this figure that are specific to your organization. There is space at the bottom of Figure 6.9 to add technical driving and restraining forces.

Figure 6.9 illustrates that there are some industry-wide technical issues remaining that restrain the adoption of SOAs, but those issues will diminish and, over time, the remaining restraining forces will be typical business and design issues.

This is not to diminish the business and design issues. They are not necessarily easy to solve, but they are the stuff of what developing an architecture is all about. Essentially, each organization must decide if it makes business sense to create an SOA using Web services. If it does, then there are design issues that need to be addressed.

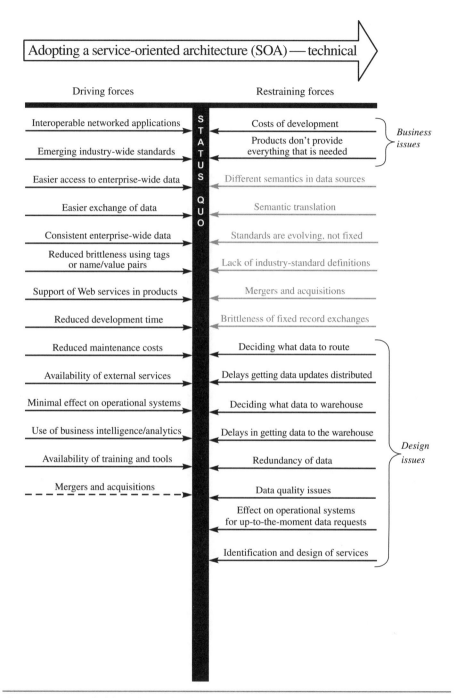

Figure 6.9 Force field analysis of technical issues related to adopting an SOA.

Summary

This chapter focused on the technical change issues related to the adoption of a service-oriented architecture. It analyzed integration techniques that preceded SOAs and the ESB, which is often used in SOAs. At the end of the chapter, the analyses were assembled into a combined force field analysis of the technical change issues for adopting an SOA using Web services. The discussion showed that by combining these integration techniques:

- The standardization efforts related to the use of Web services are assisting other integration techniques. This was shown in the weakening restraining forces for adopting an enterprise data warehouse and for ORB middleware.
- Because the use of Web services does not require abandoning existing systems or data storage, this further reduces barriers to the adoption of an SOA as part of an integration strategy.
- There are many driving forces for adopting SOAs.
- Over time, many technical restraining forces will diminish and the remaining restraining forces will be typical business and design issues.

Chapter 7

Technical Forces Driving the Adoption of Cloud Computing

Contents

This chapter provides force field analyses for adopting two types of cloud providers: software as a service (SaaS) and platform as a service (PaaS). Towards the end of the chapter, the analyses will be combined with the analysis for service-oriented architectures (SOAs). I will show that using cloud computing generally increases the number of technical driving forces for adopting an SOA. Cloud computing also increases the strength of some of the existing technical driving forces for adopting an SOA.

Adopting Software as a Service (SaaS)

There have been many examples of SaaS cloud providers[1] in this book. The audio-video (AV) example at the beginning of Chapter 4 uses multiple SaaS cloud providers. The story of C. R.'s trip mentions the customer relationship management (CRM) service that resides in the public cloud.

Figure 7.1 illustrates the driving and restraining forces for adopting SaaS. For this analysis, the forces affecting the adoption of an SOA are not included. This analysis looks at only SaaS. Including SaaS in an SOA will be analyzed later in this chapter.

Some of the forces affecting the adoption of SaaS are similar to adopting any software package. These appear in the upper right in Figure 7.1. There are restraining forces such as the service might not do everything that is needed and you may feel uncomfortable depending on a particular service. It would be reasonable to be concerned whether the service provider will keep up with new features or capabilities needed for effective use of a CRM service, for example. Also, conversion to a new system, whether in the cloud or not, can be a restraining force.

Other restraining forces are shaded in gray in Figure 7.1 to indicate they diminish with time. The first one is security. Security is often one of the biggest concerns when considering a move to a cloud provider. If you look to the left side, you will see security is a driving force as well. The reality is that major cloud providers might be more secure than a data center run by your organization. Cloud providers can hire the best security people because security is so important and the security provided is usually cutting edge. Cloud providers certainly can be targets for security attacks, but all this really does keep the security as high as possible. Since the data centers for major cloud providers are so big, they can keep equipment and software up to date because of economies of scale. Availability or uptime of a service and the Internet is similar to security. This appears on both sides in Figure 7.1. Just like security, cloud providers have the equipment and expertise to maximize availability and Internet availability will continue to improve. Both security and availability restraining forces will diminish over time, effectively increasing security and availability as driving forces for the adoption of SaaS like a CRM service.

Mergers and acquisitions might be a restraining force if the organizations use differing services or a system for something like CRM. On the other hand, the organizations might use the same service. Another option is that some industries may quickly move to a common semantic vocabulary, making a merger or acquisition less of a restraining force. In fact, Figure 7.1 shows related diminishing restraining forces, such as different semantics in data sources, semantic translation, and standards are still evolving. These are all related to standards.

---

[1]See page 42 for a discussion of PaaS.

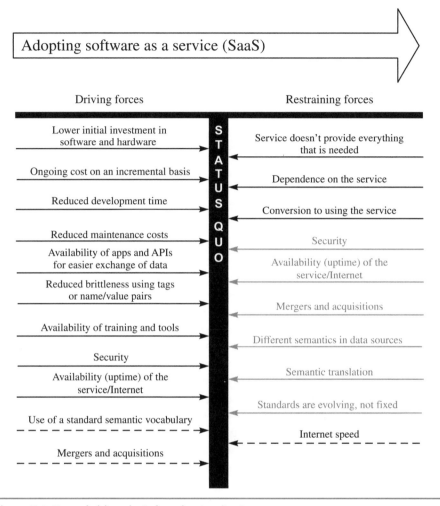

Figure 7.1 Force field analysis for adopting SaaS.

Mergers and acquisitions along with a standard semantic vocabulary are shown as dashed lines at the lower left in Figure 7.1. This indicates that they might not apply to all organizations or industries. Similarly, Internet speed as a restraining force is shown with a dashed line because speed concerns will not be an issue for all organizations.

The remaining forces are driving forces. Some are the same as in earlier analyses. These are reduced development time, reduced maintenance, and reduced brittleness using tags or name/value pairs. Also, major SaaS cloud providers for such services as CRM offer training and tools if needed.

A new driving force is the lower initial investment in software and hardware since SaaS does not require the same upfront investment as a data center. With SaaS such costs are paid for on an incremental basis as an ongoing cost (another driving force). Also, services with an SaaS cloud provider usually have application programming interfaces (APIs) as well as applications. Both make it easier for exchanging data. The applications and APIs mean that data from the service can be accessed/updated from a mobile device as well as systems running in your data center.

Adopting Platform as a Service (PaaS)

At one point, C.R.'s organization decided to store its enterprise data in the cloud instead of in a data warehouse. The organization built the new data store using a PaaS provider. Storing data in the cloud accommodated storage needs changing over time as well as changing use/analysis of the data over time. Cloud computing provides such elasticity. This way, C.R.'s organization only pays for what it uses. With cloud computing, it is not necessary for C.R.'s organization to invest in the hardware and software needed to handle peak use.

Let's assume a database management system was used in the cloud and that C.R.'s organization wrote custom software around the database management system. Also assume the PaaS provider has business intelligence (BI)/analytics software that works with the database management system.

Like many organizations, C.R.'s organization saw remarkable growth in the amount of data it maintains. To handle that amount of data, it chose a big data solution offered by a PaaS provider. *Big data* is a somewhat fuzzy term that refers to large and complicated data sets that may not be easily managed by traditional database management systems. A big data solution offered by a PaaS provider might be a NoSQL[2] database management system. There are a variety of NoSQL database management systems on the market. Most are designed to work with big data.

Figure 7.2 shows the analysis for adopting a PaaS for implementing a big data storage solution in the cloud. Many of the same forces shown in Figure 6.3 for an enterprise data warehouse also apply here. These are the restraining forces of development costs: deciding what data to store, possible delays in getting data to the data store, issues related to the redundancy of data that is stored in multiple locations, and possible data quality issues for the data being stored. The driving forces include easier access to enterprise-wide data, reduced maintenance costs, reduced brittleness using tags or name/value pairs, minimal effect on operational systems, and the use of BI/analytics.

---

[2] NoSQL is usually defined as "not only SQL."

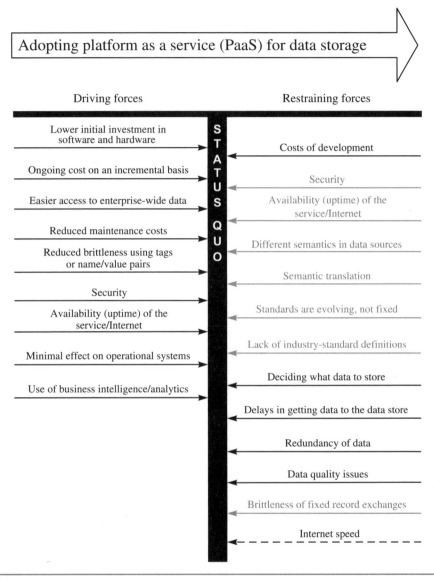

Figure 7.2 Force field analysis for adopting PaaS.

The discussion of security and availability (uptime) of the service/Internet discussed in earlier for the adoption of an SaaS also applies here. The remaining diminishing forces were discussed on page 59 for adopting an enterprise data warehouse or in the discussion for adopting SaaS earlier in this chapter.

Just as in adopting a SaaS, there are driving forces of lower initial investment in software and hardware and ongoing cost on an incremental basis. The PaaS cloud provider manages the hardware and provides the software.

Adopting Service-Oriented Architecture with Cloud Computing

It is possible to have an SOA without cloud computing. At the end of Chapter 6, SOA was analyzed without any reference to cloud computing. It is also possible to use cloud computing without an SOA. For example, my AV system illustrated in Figures 4.1 and 4.2 uses SaaS cloud providers, but my AV system is in no way a service-oriented architecture.

This section discusses SOA with cloud computing using the SaaS and PaaS examples. Figure 7.3 shows the cloud computing providers for the CRM service and the big data store. The CRM service is from a public SaaS cloud provider. The big data store along with the BI/analytics uses a virtual private PaaS cloud provider. The remaining internal systems are the same ones as were shown in Figure 6.7.

The PaaS includes tools to help develop, manage, and analyze the data in big data stores. It provides an enterprise service bus (ESB) that is optimized for the big data store and the BI/analytics software.

The Internet is represented by the horizontal shaded area. Web services are shown as a black line within the shaded area. This represents that Web services protocols (SOAP, REST, JSON, etc.) are a subset of the protocols that can be used on the Internet.

Note the adapters aligned with the big data, BI/analytics, and the CRM in the cloud. They are needed because those services use a somewhat different semantic vocabulary than the one used by C. R.'s organization.

Figure 7.4 shows the technical driving and restraining forces for adopting an SOA with cloud computing. This basically adds forces related to cloud computing to Figure 6.9, which showed the driving and restraining forces for adopting an SOA. Figure 7.4 combines forces in Figure 6.9 with the forces related to adopting an SaaS CRM service (see Figure 7.1) and PaaS to store big data and provide BI/analytics (see Figure 7.2).

In this analysis, the enterprise data warehouse was replaced with a big data store. So, the restraining forces for adopting an enterprise data warehouse (see Figure 6.3) have been reworded for storing big data (see Figure 7.2): deciding what data to store and delays in getting data to the data store. Two business issues have been added: dependence on cloud-based services and conversions to use cloud-based services. A legal issue was added concerning contractual issues with the cloud provider.[3] There is a new possible design restraint of Internet speed.

---

[3] See page 165 for more on legal issues related to cloud providers.

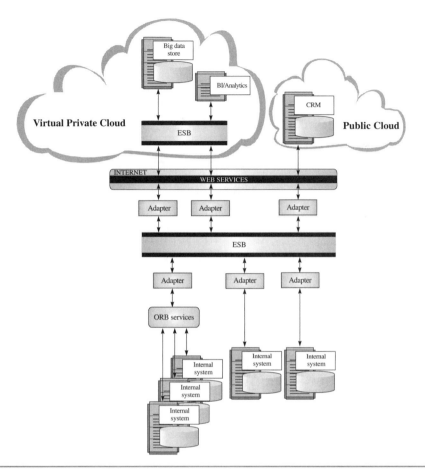

Figure 7.3 Internal systems with cloud computing for a big data store and a CRM service.

Security and availability (uptime) are both diminishing restraining forces and driving forces, as described for both SaaS and PaaS earlier in this chapter. In addition to security and availability (uptime), other new driving forces related to cloud computing are lower initial investment in software and hardware, ongoing cost on an incremental basis, and the possibility of using a standard semantic vocabulary.

Some of the driving forces related to SOAs are likely made stronger with cloud computing; they are reduced development time, reduced maintenance costs, availability of external services, and the availability of applications and APIs for easier exchange of data.

Over time, the remaining restraining forces will be typical business, legal, and design issues. Adding cloud computing generally increases the number of technical driving

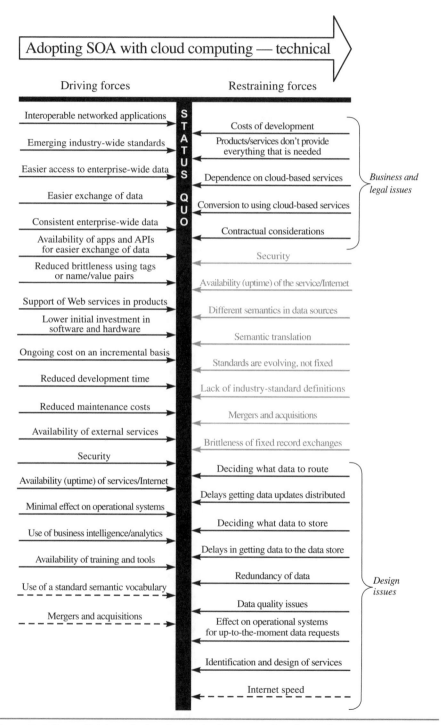

Figure 7.4 Force field analysis of technical issues related to adopting an SOA with cloud computing.

forces for adopting a service-oriented architecture. Cloud computing also increases the strength of some of the existing technical driving forces for adopting an SOA.

Summary

This chapter used force field analysis to show how various forces drive or restrain the adoption of services from two representative SaaS and PaaS cloud providers. The SaaS cloud provider was a CRM service and the PaaS cloud provider had a platform supporting big data and BI/analytics. The major finding of this analysis is that using cloud computing generally increases the number of technical driving forces for adopting an SOA. Cloud computing also increases the strength of some of the existing technical driving forces for adopting an SOA.

PART III

Managing Change Needed for Web Services, Service-Oriented Architectures, and Cloud Computing

Moving to a service-oriented architecture with cloud computing will be a significant change for many organizations. Such change must be managed properly, which involves considering the organization as a whole, the technology to be used, and the people involved in the change.

The three chapters in the previous part of the book focused on technical forces driving the adoption of Web services, service-oriented architectures, and cloud computing. This part focuses on managing change that affects the people in the organization when the organization is going through that adoption process. People worry about the future of their jobs and worry about learning new tools and technologies. An organization must address these issues and concerns to achieve success.

Chapter 8 uses the force field analysis introduced in Chapter 6. It deals with managing the human aspect of the change that occurs with the adoption of a service-oriented architecture with cloud computing. Chapter 9 provides tips on how to make development easier. Chapter 10 introduces incremental SOA analysis that aims to help manage change by improving the project selection process in a way that also improves the chance of success for the selected project.

Chapter 8

Change Issues

Contents

Managing the human aspect of the change that occurs with the adoption of a service-oriented architecture (SOA) with cloud computing can be a significant challenge. Chapter 7 showed that as technology and standards evolve, technical issues diminish, leaving the remaining restraining forces related to business, legal, and design issues. This chapter shifts the focus to human change issues. These issues most often manifest themselves in resistance to change. Forms of resistance and reasons for the resistance are discussed as well as ways to address such resistance. To anchor these concepts of resistance, I have included some of my own experiences with resistance to change.

At the end of this chapter is a worksheet for laying out change issues and responses to those issues. There is also a consolidated force field analysis for adopting an SOA that builds on the analyses covered in Chapter 7.

After completing my undergraduate work, I had a job as an analyst in a government agency. This was in a research group of about 40 people. Most of us worked in one large room. One day a senior analyst decided to move some of the desks around in the large room and, without discussing it with the people involved, went right ahead with the move. Orville, one of the older analysts, was not there at the time. Orville came back to find his desk in a different spot. Finding out who made the change, Orville ran screaming at the senior analyst and literally pushed him against the wall. Orville had an emotional problem that meant he did not deal with change well at all. The senior analyst, however, could have avoided this confrontation if only he had spoken with Orville before making the changes. Surprises of this nature trigger an automatic response of fright, flight, or fight and a variety of other reactions. Orville's emotional problems probably amplified a normal response.

Change

Not everyone who has problems dealing with change has emotional problems that make transitions worse. In fact, most of us deal with change better than Orville did in this true story. Nevertheless, there are ways to make any change easier for people and for the organization in which they work. This chapter deals with human change related to adopting SOAs with cloud computing and ways to deal with that change.

Technical Change Issues Diminishing

There are multiple types of issues related to change. The drive to use Web services in an SOA with cloud computing is reducing the technical change issues. In other words, the barriers to change related to technology are diminishing. This makes the technical change easier. Figure 8.1 is from Chapter 7 and shows the technical forces affecting the adoption of an SOA with cloud computing. The gray arrows represent the technical restraining issues that will diminish as industry adopts and expands the use of this technology. Why these forces will diminish was discussed in Chapter 7.

The analysis in Figure 8.1 is interesting because it illustrates that as the technical restraining forces shown in gray diminish, we are left with technical issues related to business, legal, and general design. These are shown at the right in Figure 8.1. There are, of course, other business and design issues, but these arrows are representative of basic business and design issues facing any effort to create an SOA with cloud computing.

At the left in Figure 8.1 are the driving forces for adopting an SOA with cloud computing. The strength of these forces will vary by organization. Also, there very well might be additional driving forces for a particular organization. Nevertheless, by almost any measure, there are tremendous driving forces for the adoption of an SOA with cloud computing.

Resistance to Change

If it makes sense for your organization to develop an SOA with cloud computing, what other restraining forces need to be considered? Probably the strongest is a general resistance to change.

Resistance is a common human response to change. Resistance to change, however, may very well be the biggest issue to address in achieving an effective SOA with cloud computing.

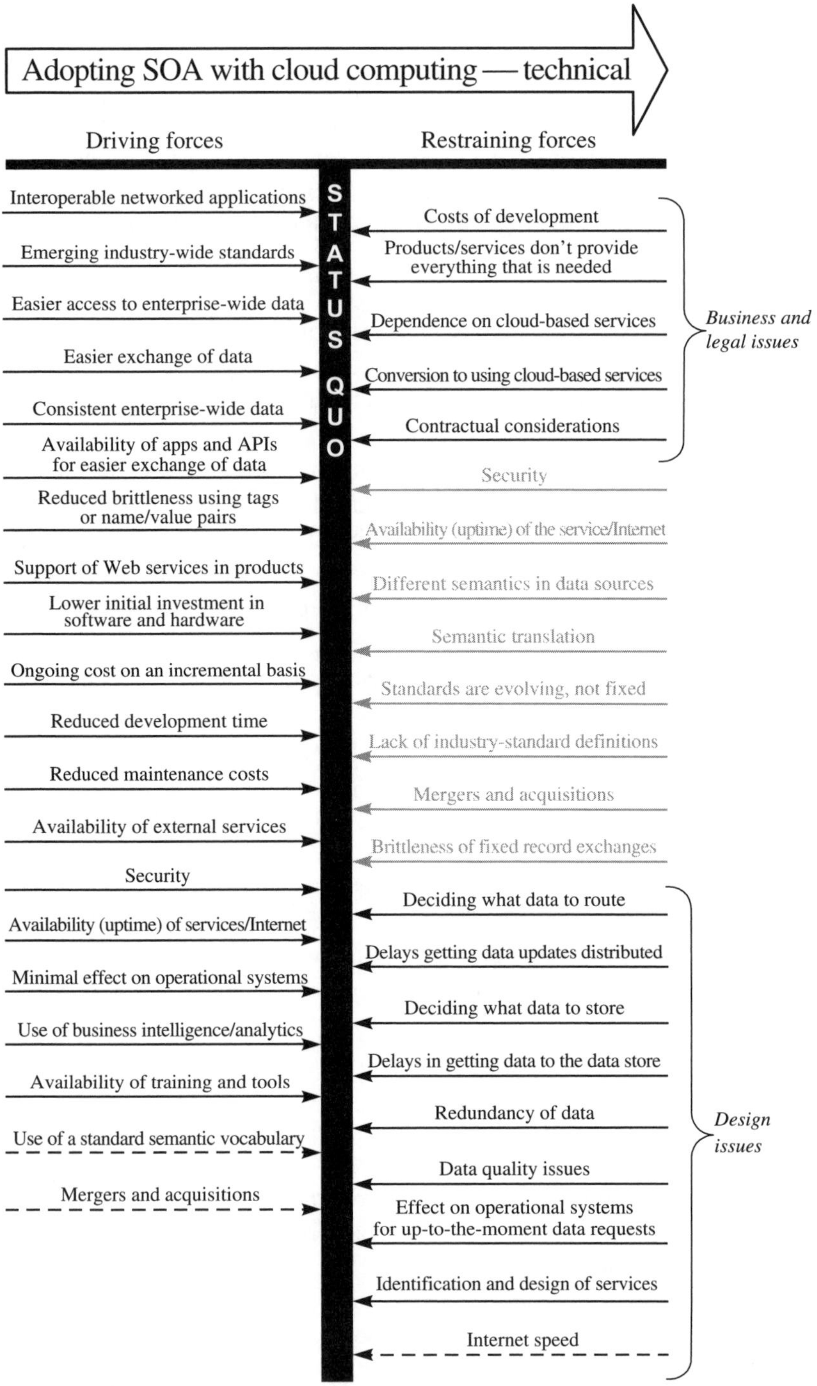

Figure 8.1 Force field analysis of technical issues related to adopting an SOA with cloud computing.

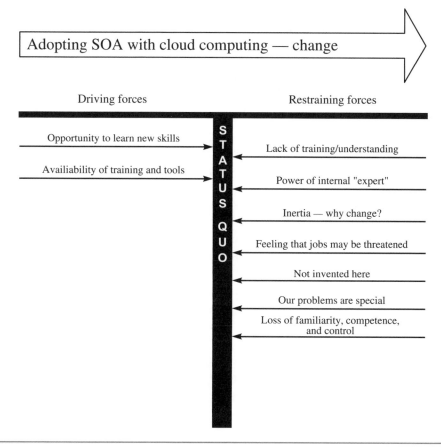

Figure 8.2 Force field analysis of change issues related to adopting an SOA.

Figure 8.2 shows the analysis of major driving and restraining forces related to change that affect the adoption of an SOA with cloud computing. There are often many restraining forces related to change. Also, if my vision of the future concerning the roles of IT staff is correct, some of the restraining forces will be stronger. For example, the restraining force of feeling that jobs may be threatened is very real as an organization moves through the process of adopting an SOA with cloud computing.[1] You may want to try adding driving and restraining forces that are specific to your organization in the space at the bottom of Figure 8.2.

As a manager, be on the lookout for resistance—where there is change, there will be resistance. The savvy manager is prepared for it and deals with it as it occurs. Some people like change and look forward to it. Those are the people who

---

[1] Many of these same forces have existed for the adoption of any technology for many years. Nevertheless, I think the expanding adoption of SOAs will have significant impact on IT organizations.

are looking for variety and they are your advocates in a technological change. There are also the folks who hate change. They may try to keep change from happening. In the middle are the "wait and see" folks. They are concerned about the impact of change on them, but they are willing to wait and see what happens. Often, this is the larger group. These are the people to focus on because you can win them to your side. Plenty of communication and participation can do wonders. The more employees worry and wonder, the stronger their resistance becomes. It's just human nature.

William Bridges has written extensively on the topic of change in organizations for the past several decades. Bridges' work, *Managing Transitions*,[2] is particularly helpful for the manager planning a technology change. His model views change as a series of events going from an ending, which is the way things used to be, to a beginning, which is the way things will be in the future when the project is complete. Between the two is the neutral zone. This is a stage in which few things are the way they were and it's not clear how they will be.

It is in the neutral zone, according to Bridges, where resistance can be found, because it is a stage that can be marked by confusion and uncertainty. In the neutral zone there are no clear markers and no promises. The savvy manager will be careful when dealing with people who may be in the neutral zone because they are seldom being difficult on purpose. They are unsure and concerned and may not realize their resistance. Sensitivity to the neutral zone is important because the manager can often help team members through this stage more quickly.

Forms of Resistance

Recognizing resistance can take some practice because many of its forms could easily be justified as a concern or a request for information. We all want employees who care enough about their work that they are willing to want to understand and state their concerns. As new projects are presented, it should be expected that employees will have many questions. In fact, one of the best things a manager can do is communicate in many ways and many times what the project entails. Some employees do better with written communication (email, blogs, websites, etc.), some with group meetings, and some with one-on-one casual conversations. All have their place in a plan for communicating change.

When a manager has communicated plans and time has passed, some team members may still be asking questions or raising concerns. Sometimes team members

---

[2] William Bridges, *Managing Transitions: Making the Most of Change* (New York: Da Capo Lifelong Books, 2009).

may be raising new concerns on a regular basis. If you have carefully considered the objections and found no grounds for the concern, this may well be a sign of resistance to change. Resistance to change in people can take many forms. Constant questioning about new concerns is a classic sign that resistance may be taking place. It also can take the shape of a form of confusion, in which the team member just can't quite get clear on how or why the project will be the way it is planned. Such a team member is probably not doing this on purpose. It's possible that this person is just not able to hear what is being communicated because of some discomfort with it. This person may well be in the neutral zone and is just trying to find his or her way through it.

Other forms of resistance may include silence or easy acceptance. People may be silent for many reasons, but it is easy to assume that silence means acceptance. That is not always the case, so be on the lookout for it. Easy acceptance can also be misleading because it may mean that the person has not considered the ramifications of the change; when he or she does think about it, you may find that this person upon whom you were counting on is no longer on board.

The following sections go into some detail on forms of resistance that were shown as restraining forces in Figure 8.2. These forms of resistance will also be referenced in the remainder of this chapter and the next two chapters.

LACK OF TRAINING/UNDERSTANDING

Sometimes people are resistant to change because they do not have the training to understand what the new project or job will entail. Many people become familiar with their job and want it to stay the same. It is particularly challenging for them if the change in their job involves new technology. Almost everyone has a concern about not measuring up in a new environment and that may well be the situation here.

A second issue in this situation is communication. Sometimes people just aren't getting the message that they need to hear. In a change situation, you can count on some people putting the most negative spin on any change. That's just human nature. In a time of uncertainty, most people will fear for the worst. That's why plenty of communication is of great importance. If people will need new training for the change, be sure they are reassured that they will get it.

Finally, the timing of training is critical. All too often, people are trained well in advance of using new technology. That is the equivalent of no training. People should be able to immediately use the new technology after training.

POWER OF INTERNAL "EXPERT"

An internal expert can be a formidable ally or a formidable roadblock in a change effort. Such an expert knows the current system and possibly the previous systems in such a way that can be of great help. On the other hand, if this person is not on board for the change effort, he or she can raise all sorts of barriers. The savvy manager needs to find a useful way to involve an internal expert in the development process.

The most probable form of resistance will be in raising concerns about the quality of the new system, and this person is likely to use his or her expert position in the organization to raise the level of recognition of the concern. It's easy to overlook what an expert has to lose in a change situation. This person is going from being an acknowledged success to a situation that is new. Because of the newness, it is impossible to know whether this person will be able to retain expert status or even if he or she will be needed in the new situation. An expert in this position may fear a loss of competence and control. That may be a big risk for such a person. This is especially true when the current expert may not have the kind of training that will make moving to the new system possible.

INERTIA—WHY CHANGE?

Sometimes it's difficult to effect change in a system just because "things" have always been done a certain way or because the system is seen as working okay. This creates a sense of inertia. People who are part of the system ask why a change is needed. This can make it difficult when the new way of doing things will create a leap forward and will bring possibilities that have not been present before. Communicating the advantages of the new options may help, but when people are comfortable in the current situation, any change can be challenging and bring resistance into play.

In fact, it may be that our brains are wired for inertia. Christopher Koch reported in *CIO Magazine*[3] on this phenomenon. He states that the:

> *"... prefrontal cortex's capacity is finite—it can deal comfortably with only a handful of concepts before bumping up against limits. That bump generates a palpable sense of discomfort and produces fatigue and even anger. That's because the prefrontal cortex is tightly linked to the primitive emotional centre of the brain, the amygdala, which controls our fight-or-flight response".*

The article goes on to explain how parts of our brain interact and why we prefer to continue doing things the same way.

FEELING THAT JOBS MAY BE THREATENED

Given the pace of technological change today, it is difficult for most people to stay knowledgeable on new technology. This means that any change may feel threatening

---

[3] Christopher Koch, "The New Science of Change," *CIO Magazine*, October 2006, http://www.cio.com. au/article/170700/new_science_change/.

to many people. Often, technology changes are put into place so that staffing can be as lean as possible. That means that not everyone will have a job after the change in technology occurs. Those people who have not kept their technical skills up may have reason to worry. Because worry tends to be contagious in an organization, most everyone will be worrying. For some people, the outlet for this worry will be resistance.

As the use of Web services is more widely adopted for making connections and you move to a service-oriented architecture, some jobs will really be threatened. We are in the process of replacing custom-coded systems with reusable services. As a manager, you will need to keep this very legitimate concern in mind when creating an SOA with cloud computing.

NOT INVENTED HERE

Most people take pride in their work. It's easy for managers to forget or not even know the blood, sweat, and tears that went into a project that was completed some time ago. The people who worked on that project do remember. When they hear that the work that they did will be replaced, there's always a sense of loss. In the excitement of bringing in the new, the organizational focus ignores the earlier contribution of the people and their project and focuses on the shortcomings of the old. This can lead to resistance on the part of those who have worked on the old system.

OUR PROBLEMS ARE SPECIAL

I've worked with many groups of people working on technology issues. Amazingly, almost all of them believed that the technical problems that they had to solve were quite complex and unusual. From my perception as an outsider, many of those same problems struck me as fairly normal for the industry that they were in or the work that they were doing. There were, of course, some twists that required attention, but those twists were not significant enough to scuttle a project.

This is a common excuse used by technical people to avoid using an off-the-shelf product or a cloud-based service. On a rare occasion it may be true, but most often it is just a means of resistance used by those who want to keep things as they are or to develop something new on their own.

LOSS OF FAMILIARITY, COMPETENCE, AND CONTROL

Neuroscience research has uncovered information that explains a great deal about resistance. According to David Rock and Jeffrey Schwartz,[4]

---

[4] David Rock and Jeffrey Schwartz, "The Neuroscience of Leadership," *Strategy + Business*, May 2006, http://www.strategy-business.com/article/06207.

Managers who understand the recent breakthroughs in cognitive science can lead and influence mindful change: organizational transformation that takes into account the physiological nature of the brain, and the ways in which it predisposes people to resist some forms of leadership and accept others.

Rock and Schwartz stress that change of any kind is a form of pain that causes serious reactions in the brain. In fact, research using magnetic resonance imaging (MRI) indicates that organizational change may be perceived by the brain as not that different from being attacked by an animal in a forest.

Change that affects a worker's sense of familiar comfort about how to do the work, being competent at it and in control of it, may be the breeding ground for the resistance that so endangers many projects. The human brain appears to process information on several levels. The familiar is processed somewhat automatically and takes less energy. New processes are perceived as possible errors and require more energy. According to Rock and Schwartz, "Trying to change any hardwired habit requires a lot of effort, in the form of attention. This often leads to a feeling that many people find uncomfortable. So they do what they can to avoid change."

Suggestions for Addressing Resistance to Change

The first step in addressing any kind of resistance to change is to recognize it for what it is. Sometimes resistance easily stops a project because it is never addressed. When the manager notices that nothing seems to be happening or that the project is far off schedule, it is past time to consider that resistance is at play.

The best bet is to anticipate resistance, even before the project starts. This means that you can set things up to avoid some of the resistance and you will be in a good situation to address it should it arise. The next sections discuss ways to address resistance to change.

SELECTING THE RIGHT PEOPLE

One key to the success of any project is careful selection of people to work on the project. Selecting a person because he or she has been around a long time isn't generally a good reason for that person to be on the team. Choosing someone because he or she doesn't currently have a project is not a good reason either. Sometimes staffing for a project is seen as a way to resolve problem personnel situations. That's also not the route to success on your project.

The best approach to selecting the right people is to identify what kind of skills and experience are needed on the project team. Then find the people in your organization who can meet those standards. Be sure these people have a positive, open mind. If people cannot be found internally, then you need to consider new hires or a contracting situation.

My experience tells me that a big factor in failed projects is a lack of people with the skills and experience required. This is something that will hinder any project. The outcome of any project can only be as successful as the skills of the people who work on it.

USE A SECOND SET OF EYES

Another practice that can be of great help in limiting resistance is pairing team members together. There are many methodologies that call for paired team members. There are excellent technical reasons to do this, but there are also reasons that will address resistance to change. Careful team selection means that you are unlikely to have both people in the pair with the same issues. That means that neither person will be left stewing on his or her own. In addition, the possibility that both people will be allowing the schedule to slip or participate in other resistant activities is less likely.

REALLY LISTEN

One of the best things that you can do with someone who you think may be experiencing resistance is to listen. By that, I mean really listen and not try to talk the person out of his or her ideas. Most of the time, what we think is listening is actually thinking about how to answer the person's objections. If you find yourself talking more than the other person, it means you aren't really listening. If you find yourself explaining things, then you aren't really listening. Some people think that just saying the same thing repeatedly will help improve understanding. When you find yourself doing this, it means that you are not hearing what the person is saying.

Sometimes what the person has identified as the problem is just the obvious surface of the real problem. It is more effective to ask the other person questions to probe into what might be behind the resistance. Ask questions such as, "What is your concern about that?" Follow up your questions with a summary such as, "So, you are concerned that if we implement this change, _____ might happen and that would be a problem because of _____." Let the person clarify your understanding until you both agree that you understand the other person's point of view.

If you listen in this way, you can even disagree with the other person, and the person will feel that he or she has been heard. People don't necessarily need agreement to feel that they've been heard.

COMMUNICATE AT MANY LEVELS

An effective antidote to resistance is communication and plenty of it. It's a human response to anticipate the bad things that may happen and a communication vacuum contributes to that.

To deal with resistance issues, regular communication in many forms is helpful. People have different styles and it's helpful to provide communication in as many forms as possible so that each style gets its needs met.

It also can be helpful to establish a communication schedule so that people can anticipate when more communication will be available to them. In fact, any promises that are made must be met. Don't overpromise and then not meet the promises. That just sets up a foundation for mistrust.

And while you're at it, think about communicating up the management chain as well. Find methods that will be reassuring to management and create a schedule that you can meet and that they can depend on. This helps protect your project from rumor and innuendo.

SEEK APPROPRIATE AVENUES TO INVOLVE PEOPLE

Participation is another important part of avoiding resistance to change. The more people feel part of something, the more they will support it. This can take a variety of forms, including asking for people's input and review. Be sure to be clear in your request for information so that people really hear the request and believe it is really wanted. I've seen situations where management asked for input and got none because employees either didn't hear it or didn't believe it. If asking for input is not a regular part of your organization's culture, you will need to ask in a variety of ways. Sometimes a casual request at the water cooler creates a more believable request than a general statement in an open meeting. And don't forget to really listen to the input and ideas.

GET RESISTANCE OUT IN THE OPEN

Naming resistance for what it is can bring it out into the open so that people can talk about it. Talking about it takes away its power to disrupt.

It's important to do this in a neutral and nonthreatening way. For example, don't point a finger and tell a person or group that they are resisting change. Such an approach is likely to make things worse—even if it is true. It's better to create a situation where people can state their resistance on their own. Hold a team meeting and create a comfortable situation by stating something like, "I'm sure you have concerns about this change. I'll bet that the new architecture is a little hard to understand in such a short time. At least I know I'd feel that way." Approaching the issue in this way will make it possible to get the issue on the table for discussion.

ASK FOR PARTICIPATION AND FORM PARTNERSHIPS

Make sure you ask for participation and ideas and truly listen and consider them. People can accept almost anything if they believe that their ideas have been taken seriously. Create a partnership where you will be sharing information on a regular basis so that participants become familiar with what the new system will be. As they gain information, try to show how their competence will be needed. The more information they have, the more control they are likely to feel about the future. If you have people who don't have the skills to be part of the future, address this with your human resource people. Leaving these people in limbo can create great negativity for the project.

Some Resistance Scenarios

This section includes scenarios from some of my own experiences with resistance to change (of course, names and details have been altered). After each scenario, resistance issues are listed and discussed. Then suggestions for addressing those resistance issues are also listed and discussed.

As you read the following scenarios, you will see certain themes emerging. The first is that resistance can take many forms and is not always immediately recognizable as resistance. The second is that the person resisting change is often not even aware of the motivation for his or her behavior.

BUT IT'S SO COMPLICATED!

As he put a team together to replace an existing system, the manager felt fortunate to be able to include a person who had worked on the existing system for over a decade. Betty was a competent programmer and had a nearly encyclopedic memory of why the existing system worked the way it did. She was also quite articulate and seemed very interested in helping to create the replacement system.

The early investigations into how the replacement system should work went well. Betty was quite helpful in making sure the team had all the details and idiosyncrasies documented. She was also very helpful when it came to designing the data model the replacement system would use.

Then something happened. As the team started to design how the software would work, Betty started to bring up new issues that should have been uncovered in the early investigations. Of course, it is understandable that some things would be overlooked, but the number of these issues became overwhelming. Sometimes, these issues required considerable rework to change what was already completed. It seemed as if Betty waited until all the rework was done before bringing up another issue. And unfortunately, sometimes these issues also required rework. Eventually, however, the team seemed to have a robust design and was able to answer many of Betty's concerns on the spot.

Then things started to get a bit weird. When team members would answer one of Betty's concerns and show her how the design took into account the issue she raised, Betty would often respond, "But it's so complicated." Betty was apparently convinced that the existing system had to be more complicated than the replacement system.

Because of her experience on the existing system, Betty had a huge following in this large organization. She was known and respected all the way up to the vice-presidential level because she had worked with these people for decades. This replacement system was also seen as critical to the organization's future. So, when Betty started moving up the management chain with her lament, "But it's so complicated," people took notice. Management started to want to know why the group was doing this inferior design and became worried about the future of the project. In fact, some vice presidents started to threaten cancellation of the project if the IT group could not do a better job on this critical replacement system. A lot of money was still allocated to completing this project and they did not want to spend that much money on an inferior replacement.

More and more time was spent on meetings with upper management. The system designers and analysts all had to attend numerous meetings. In those meetings, Betty brought up issue after issue concerning how much more complicated the existing system was compared to the proposed system. The dynamic was interesting. The issues Betty brought up were often in terms that management could understand. The explanation of how the proposed system would handle the issues often had to be in terms of data models and software architecture. Many people in management honestly did not understand the more technical explanations, so they were left with the impression that Betty might have a point.

Time passed. Development slowed. Eventually, the project was canceled. Sometime later, a packaged product was brought in to replace the existing system. But as you might expect, Betty at first thought the packaged product would work only to later discover that the packaged product needed much modification, because the existing system was so "complicated." That project was also canceled.

Resistance Issues in This Scenario

- Lack of training/understanding
- Power of internal "expert"
- Inertia—why change?

- Feeling that jobs may be threatened
- Our problems are special
- Loss of familiarity, competence, and control

Every technical change has incredible impact on the people involved with both the new and old systems. In fact, every change of this type has winners and losers. As development proceeds, people sometimes change camps.

In this scenario, Betty had worked hard over the years with the current system. She was emotionally invested in it and was very impressed with how well it worked and how important her role was. Because of her years of experience, she had created a strong network of personal advocates for her point of view. Initially, she may have been sure that no new system could possibly replace the system that she knew was very complicated, so she was willing to work on the team to replace it. In fact, she had already been on several committees in the past that had put the kibosh on replacements because the existing system, and of course the work that it had to do, was so complicated. In this particular situation, she was willing to participate and cooperate on the team until it dawned on her that this replacement system might actually happen. Then she began to raise issue after issue. When this happened, it became apparent that on some level she had begun to feel challenged in her position as the resident expert. I don't believe that Betty knew she felt this way. I think she was challenged as an expert on a deep level. The rest is history. Betty used all of her connections to stop this project. Upper management can be notoriously fearful of failure and Betty's concerns fed right into that. Sometimes it may seem that anybody can kill a project because of any "issue," while it's very hard to get enough people or the right people to back it.

Suggestions for Addressing Resistance

- Really listen
- Communicate at many levels
- Seek appropriate avenues to involve people
- Get resistance out in the open
- Ask for participation and form partnerships

The most important issue in this scenario is to recognize the human issues that come with change. This has implications both for the people doing the work and management supporting the work.

Technical people generally approach others in the organization—and questions within the IT organization—from a technical perspective. While technical questions must have technical answers, there are other issues at stake that, left unanswered, will sink a project. In this case, Betty's issues were not technical—they were personal. The closer implementation came, the nearer she was to losing her standing as the resident expert. So, naturally, the old system—her system—became more and more complicated in her mind and irreplaceable.

From the start, listening to Betty should have been important, but, beyond that, *finding an important role for her in the new project should have been critical.* Because she had connections in upper management, perhaps she could have served as communication person in the project, and an implementation role for the replacement system would have been important. The new system would have required training for employees, which might have been a good spot for her. Granted, finding the right role might be challenging and might require some coaching or mentoring to get her up to speed, but the alternative, in this case, was a failed project.

A second issue was not getting management on board. Betty was able to cancel a project through a whisper campaign to her old buddies in management. This indicates that management was not properly briefed or brought on board at the beginning of the project, nor were they kept informed properly during development. This is another situation where technical people may oversell the technical answer and not carefully communicate, on a regular basis, the information that can be understood. The very technical answers that can be so important and interesting to technical people may put off management who do not understand their significance. This means learning to go beyond the technology to what the technology will do for the organization. What are the outcomes that will make a difference to them? This should be the focus of technical/management discussions. When this occurs, a project will be less vulnerable to a whisper campaign.

GUERILLA TACTICS

One of the best technical minds in the company, Nancy was given the responsibility of designing and implementing the integration of two systems critical to her organization. The integration was somewhat controversial, with some seeing it as necessary and others thinking it was the wrong direction. Nancy stated that she was in favor of the integration and was given the responsibility for completing the project. She put together a small team and set to work on the problem. For many in the organization, this seemed to be about a two-month project. Nancy concurred.

At the two-month point, the project was not done. Nancy assured everyone that it was well on its way. At four months, it was still not done. Again, Nancy said that it was being properly handled; there were just a few glitches. At seven months, the project was canceled.

Resistance Issues in This Scenario

- Power of internal "expert"
- Inertia—why change?
- Loss of familiarity, competence, and control

What happened? It turned out that Nancy really enjoyed working on the fringes of technology. She found some academic research that seemed to fit this problem quite well. Her team enjoyed working on the fringes of technology as well. They put together quite an elegant plan that involved writing significant amounts of code. Never mind that you could buy portions of the solution. Hooking that into the full solution would be less elegant. Given her status in the company, little oversight was maintained on any work she did.

What really happened? Although she had stated that she supported the integration project, Nancy did not think it was the right direction for her company. She may not have even been aware that she was using her emphasis on the elegant solution as a way to kill the project, but that's what happened.

Resistance is an emotional reaction that can leave people unaware of the motivations for their actions.

Suggestions for Addressing Resistance

- Selecting the right people
- Use a second set of eyes
- Seek appropriate avenues to involve people
- Get resistance out in the open
- Ask for participation and form partnerships

Managing brilliant, creative people has been a challenge since management began. Harnessing that capability in a way that will benefit the organization can be overwhelmingly difficult. In this particular case, Nancy either was not the right person for the job or she was not managed properly. Selecting the right people for the tasks in a technology project may be the most critical decision, but it is often less studied than the hardware and software to be used. Nancy's interest in the fringes of technology could be very helpful to an organization, but in this case it killed a critical, yet constrained, two-month project. Her management should have foreseen this problem and could have either had someone else head the project or paired Nancy with someone who could steer her brilliance in a more pragmatic direction.

Second, Nancy and her organization were unaware of her true feelings about this project. Managers need to be on the lookout for signs of resistance. When things just don't add up, resistance may be in play. Managers need to assess how things are going and be ready to make changes. Nancy's manager should have taken a closer look at the project on an ongoing basis. Checking in at two months, when the project was to have been completed, was too late. Using standard project management techniques, a detailed schedule should have been developed and checkpoints, perhaps on a weekly basis, should have been observed. Activities such as design walkthroughs, code reviews, or inspections might also have helped. Given Nancy's interest in the fringes of technology and her possible resistance, these checkpoints should have been quite in depth. This would have flagged the slowing schedule early on and changes could have been made.

More Guerilla Tactics

Todd had almost single-handedly built the company's master record system. In fact, he had also been involved in the construction of two successive generations of the master record system. He had the respect of nearly everyone in the company. In this case, that respect was so high that he was seen as a systems guru. Todd agreed that it was once again time to upgrade the master record system. The present system was not fast enough and cost too much to maintain. Todd saw this as an opportunity to improve on his previous designs.

What Todd had built, however, was now available from numerous software vendors. Some of those vendors could legitimately show that their packaged software products could significantly outperform the system that Todd had designed. A technical review of the capabilities of the packaged software products showed, to most everyone's satisfaction, that the software could perform as needed. But not for Todd. In meetings, he often brought up arcane issues. When asked to document them, he agreed. But it never happened and given his standing in the organization, his lack of follow-through was overlooked. More meetings would bring more concerns. To everyone on the development team, it was becoming clear that Todd had never been satisfied with the master records systems he had designed and that he wanted one more chance to do it "right." The packaged software option would take away his opportunity.

Todd and the CEO of the company were close friends and had both been with the company from its start. Eventually, this relationship allowed Todd to recreate his master record system. It may not surprise you that the new system is still not as fast as the packaged system and requires more maintenance.

Resistance Issues in This Scenario

- Not invented here
- Power of internal "expert"
- Feeling that jobs may be threatened
- Our problems are special
- Loss of familiarity, competence, and control

This scenario illustrates a huge shift that has already occurred in the software business. Not that many years ago, most organizations had to rely on a systems guru and a large staff inside the organization who could design unique applications to meet the organization's unique needs. Now many products and services can be used as is or augmented to meet the organization's needs. This is a huge opportunity for organizations to trim the cost of new systems.

The scenario does, however, point out the significant people issues involved in this kind of change. The huge change is not only in the software but also in the staffing needs that organizations will have in this situation. Gurus, like Todd, just won't be needed on an ongoing basis any more. They may be needed on the front-end design stage, but that will be it.

This shift has huge issues for organizations in a number of ways. As in the earlier case of Betty, Todd was bringing up arcane issues that seemed outside of the satisfactory technical reviews that were taking place. This should be a clue to management that resistance may be part of the picture. Todd may not be aware of his personal interest in redesigning the system, but it does appear that this was a wasted opportunity for the organization.

Suggestions for Addressing Resistance

- Selecting the right people
- Use a second set of eyes
- Get resistance out in the open
- Ask for participation and form partnerships

The challenge for management is to find a way that Todd's abilities can be used in a positive way, rather in the negative way that has emerged in this situation. If no answer can be found, it is probably better for Todd that he move on before his technical skills become out of date. Although his relationship with the CEO might seem to make him invulnerable to change, a better point of view would be to use that relationship to help him find a fit where his skills would be of use.

THE ELEPHANT IN THE ROOM

George was a vice president of benefits who saw his organization as excelling at providing specific internal services to its employees. He wanted a system that, as he described it, would be the "Cadillac of systems" to support those services. Having established himself as an internationally recognized expert in this area of internal employee services, he had convinced upper management to fund this effort.

Early on, an outside consultant was brought in by the IT department to help define the needs of this internal system. It was clear to the consultant that there were several commercial systems on the market that would easily support the needs of these internal systems. The IT department told the consultant to not bring up this possibility because it was important to George to build his own system and George was a vice president. In fact, George saw the organization eventually selling his "Cadillac system" to other organizations.

Building such a system was more expensive than buying one on the market. No one in IT, however, ever brought up the idea of buying a commercial product rather than building one. While this system was being built, the organization's income decreased significantly in areas independent of the development effort. As a result, it was determined that it did not make sense to spend this much money on such a fancy internal system. The project was canceled after already spending many times more money than a commercial product would have cost.

Resistance Issues in This Scenario

■ Not invented here
■ Power of internal "expert"
■ Our problems are special
■ Loss of familiarity, competence, and control

Telling the truth about technology can be a politically painful event, especially when people in high places are the people who need the message. Many a manager has had to deal with a "pet project" of upper management.

Suggestions for Addressing Resistance

■ Communicate at many levels
■ Get resistance out in the open
■ Ask for participation and form partnerships

This is a case when "managing up" would be a good idea. In this scenario, no one even raised the idea that commercially available software might work as well. Carefully planting the idea that this is possible could have been done in such a way that the VP would get the message clearly. The VP's need to have a special product might also have been addressed on another project.

Worksheet for Resistance Issues and Suggestions

The scenarios above provide some examples of resistance issues and the possible suggestions for addressing those issues. Of course, you may have other resistance issues in your organization that may benefit from different sorts of responses. Figure 8.3 provides a worksheet you can use to think about restraining forces you may have added to Figure 8.2 and possible suggestions you could consider.

Consolidated Analysis for Adopting an SOA with Cloud Computing

Figure 8.4 consolidates the driving and restraining technical forces from Figure 8.1 and the driving and restraining forces related to change from Figure 8.2. The restraining technical forces that will fade away over time (the ones shown in gray in Figure 8.1)

have been removed from this analysis. Figure 8.4 shows that using Web services reduces
the technical issues restraining the adoption of SOAs with cloud computing and leaves

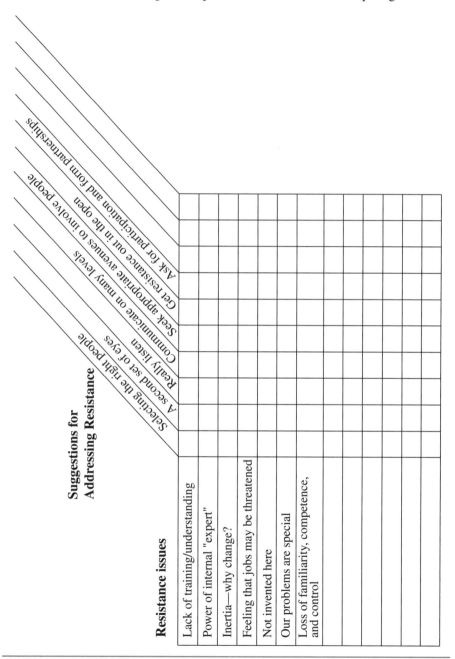

Figure 8.3 Resistance issues and suggestions worksheet.

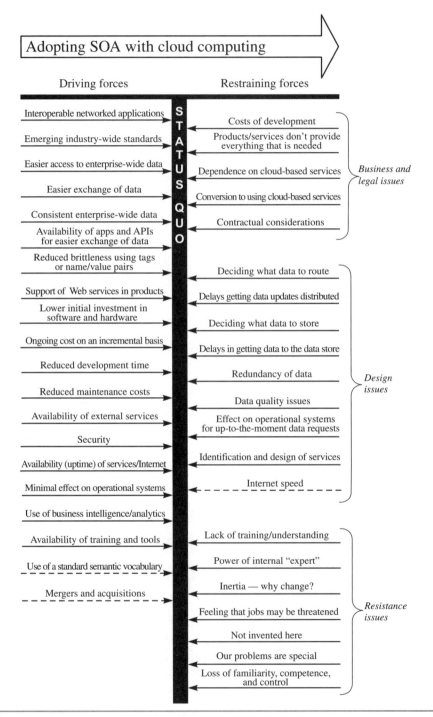

Figure 8.4 Force field analysis for adopting an SOA with cloud computing.

business, legal, design, and resistance issues. Business, legal, and design issues will always be with us. Resistance issues will form the biggest obstacles to the adoption of SOAs with cloud computing.

Summary

The use Web services is rapidly removing many of the technical restraining forces related to adopting an SOA with cloud computing. At the same time, these technologies are adding technical driving forces toward adoption. As a result, the primary restraining forces within organizations for adoption of SOAs have to do with business, legal, and design issues—and human resistance to change. Business, legal, and design issues are part of developing any architecture. Change issues, however, could trip up the adoption of an SOA. Ways to identify and address resistance were covered in this chapter along with scenarios of various forms of resistance. Chapter 9 will expand on dealing with resistance by providing some tips for managing change issues.

Tips for Managing Change Issues During Development

Contents

As with any human endeavor, there are easy ways and hard ways to do anything. This chapter provides tips on how to make development easier. These tips come from my development and consulting experiences. They are not intended to be comprehensive. Nevertheless, they just might help you with managing change issues during development.

Design as Little as Possible

If you haven't experienced "analysis paralysis," you are a rare member of our profession. The design of a system can sometimes seem as if it will go on forever. The best tip I can give you is to design as little as possible. It may sound counterintuitive, but most of the successful projects I have seen are based on as little design as possible. How do you do this? One way is to buy a system or use one or more existing services. Another way is to buy a model or adopt a semantic vocabulary. Any of these tips will narrow the amount of design that you must do.

BUY A SYSTEM OR USE ONE OR MORE EXISTING SERVICES

When you buy a system or use one or more existing services, you are essentially leveraging existing software that you can plug into your overall architecture. Doing this will reduce your design work. You can focus on the connections in your architecture and the unique parts of your architecture that you must design. When considering any type of software, be sure that it can participate in a service-oriented architecture (SOA). As Web services are adopted throughout our industry, it will also become increasingly possible to buy "plug-compatible" software components or use cloud-based services that you can assemble into an SOA.

The change issues you will likely encounter are:

- **Feeling that jobs may be threatened.** Yes, in many cases they might be. You will need to plan for this eventuality.
- **Our problems are special.** Yes, there are probably some special problems, but should they be driving your development? In the rare case, I have seen this to be true. In most organizations, however, there aren't special problems and if you look at the problems in a different way, it is possible to see how existing software or services can address those problems.

BUY A MODEL OR ADOPT A SEMANTIC VOCABULARY

If there are good reasons to not buy software, you don't need to start with a clean sheet of paper. There are data models available for purchase that are applicable to most segments of industry. Often these are referred to as *universal data models*. Universal data models can work with both data warehouses/master databases or with big data in the cloud. Similarly, there are semantic vocabularies designed for specific industries.

I cannot begin to tell you how many times I have seen people struggling to model the same data or vocabularies where data models or semantic vocabularies already exist. Frankly, how many different ways are there to model customers, employees, addresses, products, and so on? Yes, there are variations among companies. Nevertheless, if you look at the universal data models or semantic vocabularies, many of those variations are handled in elegant ways. In fact, usually experienced data modelers develop the universal data models and semantic vocabularies—often these folks are more experienced than any modelers you might find in your organization. Months—yes, months—of modeling efforts in an organization fall short of almost any universal model or semantic vocabulary. If you need to add something to an existing model or vocabulary, it is usually a minor addition requiring minor modeling.

The change issues you will likely encounter are:

- **Lack of training/understanding**. The fact of the matter is that when confronted with a universal data model or standard semantic vocabulary, many people don't see how it will work. Often, it is because they are stuck in their view of how the system should work, based on what they have experienced. They are often trying to "map" their understanding of the current system to the universal data model vocabulary. This can be a stretch for some people.
- **Power of the internal "expert."** Oh my goodness—bringing in a universal model or semantic vocabulary can really threaten this person. Telling anyone that these things will be better than something that this person—an expert after all—could put together is a very difficult sell. You will need to plan for significant resistance here. Chapter 8 provides some suggestions.
- **Not invented here**. It is really tough to realize that other people have actually addressed many of your modeling issues. Even worse is the possibility that someone else may have done a better job.
- **Our problems are special**. This might be true around the fringes of a universal data model or semantic vocabulary. In a rare case, it might be true in general. Be sure to thoroughly search before accepting that your problems are truly special.

Write as Little Code as Possible

This sounds too easy, but it is true. Time and again, I see people writing more code than necessary. Couple this with the fact that on average, professional coders make 100–150 errors per thousand lines of code,[1] and you want to write as little code as possible just to minimize the errors.

---

[1] Watts S. Humphrey, in a Multiyear study of 13,000 programs conducted by the Software Engineering Institute, Carnegie Mellon. Mentioned in "Why Software Is So Bad... and What's Being Done to Fix It," Charles C. Mann, *MSNBC Technology Review*, June 27, 2002.

Of course, buying systems, buying models, or using existing services will reduce the code you write. You should consider those options first. As Web services continue to be adopted throughout our industry, it will become increasingly possible to buy "plug-compatible" software components that you can assemble into an SOA.

If you have to write code, take a serious look at the systems you have. How many times have you written the same code to validate a customer account? I know some managers who have been able to identify the relatively few procedures they have that have been written repeatedly. Factor those out. You might be surprised by how much reusable code you have.

Reduce Project Scope

Many development methodologies emphasize reduced project scope and reduced project times. Nevertheless, it is so tempting to create big projects. You and your team need to come up with ways to minimize the scope of each project. Multiyear projects are unthinkable. Twelve-month projects should be looked at skeptically. The challenge to the manager is to create projects that can be completed in less than 12 months—less than 3 months would be even better.

Smaller projects are more focused and are more likely to succeed. Large projects are likely to fail. Since 1994, the Standish Group has conducted studies on IT development projects, compiling the results in the *Chaos Reports*. In 2005, Watts S. Humphrey of the Software Engineering Institute looked at the Standish Group's data by project size. His research showed that half of the smaller projects succeeded, whereas none of the largest projects did.[2]

Related to reducing project scope is the idea of building an SOA incrementally. Chapter 10 provides specific suggestions in this area.

Use a Methodology

In all my years of consulting, I have only rarely encountered companies that are really using any software methodology. Sure, they may say they are, but in reality they are still "shooting from the hip" when developing software.

---

[2] Watts S. Humphrey, "Why Big Software Projects Fail: The 12 Key Questions." *CrossTalk: The Journal of Defense Software Engineering,* March 2005.

Any methodology is better than no methodology. Yes, you can argue as to one being better than another, but the plain fact of the matter is that if you truly follow any methodology, you are going to be much better off than when just paying lip service to the methodology or simply not using one.[3]

To take advantage of a methodology, invest in a tool that supports the methodology. Paper systems or drawing tools that are not integrated with the methodology often end up being not very helpful. Not using a tool lets people "cheat" or not stick to the "rules" of a methodology.

Use a Second Set of Eyes

Many methodologies involve having at least one other person look at any particular piece of work. Using a "second set of eyes" is critical. The trick, however, is really using a second set of eyes. Have you been in a group code review where the programmer describes what is going on in the program and everyone more or less nods their way through the review? How helpful is that really? Methodologies that require someone other than the author to describe what is going on in an architecture, design, program, and so on are much more effective. It requires that person's second set of eyes to really look and that second mind to really understand.

Use Small Teams

For years I have been recommending that people should consider the communication issues in software development to be much like a dinner party. When you have a dinner party of seven or less, it is usually possible to have one conversation. As soon as you have eight or more people at the table, the dinner party breaks into two conversations and no one hears everything that was said.

This is often what happens in software development. Communication is critical. Use a small team. Put them together in a one room. Let them focus on development of their project; that means that the project is the only thing they are doing.

---

[3] One person who reviewed this manuscript for the first edition of the book commented that methodologies could be used as another form of resistance. He described how entrenched experts in an organization can use methodologies as a covert means to ensure a project gets nowhere because of "the demands of the methodology." A variant of this would be using methodologies inappropriate for an organization, thereby slowing development. I guess you need to be ever vigilant to resistance issues.

Summary

As stated at the outset of this chapter, these tips came from my development and consulting experience. They are meant to improve your chances of being successful with your development efforts. Chapter 10 uses three tools that address change issues.

Managing Change with Incremental SOA Analysis

Contents

Service-oriented architecture (SOA) projects are no different from other IT projects in that larger projects tend to fail and issues regarding change can scuttle projects. This chapter introduces incremental SOA analysis. It aims to improve the project selection process in a way that also improves the chance of success for the selected project. This analysis takes into account both project size and the human change issues discussed in the previous two chapters.

The incremental SOA analysis uses three tools that address change issues. Two of the tools were discussed in earlier chapters: force field analysis and the resistance issues and suggestions worksheets. This chapter introduces a third tool: the decomposition matrix. The tools are intended to engage people in such a way that they can come to their own resolution on what might be causing human change issues.

Tools

People are much more likely to deal better with change issues if they are engaged in the change process. Chapter 8 suggested possible ways to address change issues. Of those suggestions, the three tools used in this chapter allow you to:

- Use a second set of eyes
- Really listen
- Communicate at many levels
- Seek appropriate avenues to involve people
- Get resistance out in the open
- Ask for participation and form partnerships

It is important to try using all three tools in a group setting—with the appropriate participants, of course. The tools are intended to get people talking and, hopefully, thinking differently about their design work.

FORCE FIELD ANALYSIS

Chapters 5–7 discussed force field analysis. It engages people in the process of identifying change issues. Force field analysis can be used in a group setting if you use something like a whiteboard or flip chart.

WORKSHEET FOR RESISTANCE ISSUES AND SUGGESTIONS

The worksheet for resistance issues and suggestions introduced in Chapter 8 also allows a group to problem solve. As with force field analysis, the worksheets can be used with whiteboards or flip charts. The worksheets start with the resistance issues identified in the force field analysis.

A significant issue when making any systems change, particularly in large organizations, is getting agreement on what the changed system should do. This compounds the situation where it is often difficult to see how the changed system should be. Not only might individuals have a difficult time thinking of how their workflow could be different, there might be entirely different views of the workflow in different parts of an organization. A tool like the decomposition matrix can be a way to address different views within an organization by getting people to only think about inputs, outputs, and how they relate to each other.

DECOMPOSITION MATRIX

The decomposition matrix tool generates either business process or data flow diagrams. It does this using an algebra for design decomposition that Mike Adler published in the 1980s.[1]

A feature of the decomposition matrix is that it does not look at all like a business process or data flow diagram. Business process diagrams, for example, are a great way to design a workflow. The problem for most of us, however, is that if we are familiar with a given workflow, it is often difficult to see how it could be significantly different. We all tend to repeat or recreate what we know. The decomposition matrix, however, requires us to only think about inputs, outputs, and how they relate to each other. The diagrams are generated for you based on the matrix of inputs, outputs, and relationships.

I have the decomposition matrix tool implemented on one of my websites.[2] It is free to use. It can be used in a group setting if you have a computer with an Internet connection hooked up to a projector.

Figure 10.1 shows a decomposition matrix of inputs, outputs, and relationships. It allows you to discuss detailed issues one at a time instead of trying to juggle multiple issues all together in a design. You only need to make a series of binary decisions. Such a decision is whether a given input is related to a given output. Sometimes that can generate a great deal of discussion and bring out design issues not previously mentioned. The decomposition matrix assembles these simple decisions and generates a decomposition that might help you with your design process.

---

[1] Mike Adler, "An Algebra for Data Flow Diagram Process Decomposition," *IEEE Transactions on Software Engineering*, 14(2), (Feb. 1988).

[2] "Design Decomposition for Business Process and Data Flow Diagrams," Barry & Associates, *http://www.designdecomposition.com/*.

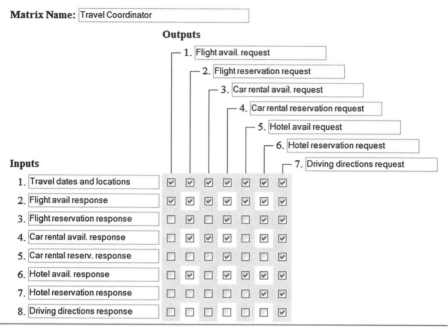

Figure 10.1 Decomposition matrix example.

The tool on my website generates either business process or data flow diagrams. Most people are familiar with business process diagrams. The data flow diagrams are a way to get at the decomposition of services in an SOA. The decomposition matrix has a specific definition of atomicity. *Atomicity* generally means that a business process cannot be decomposed further (see page 17 for a general definition of atomic services). The specific definition of atomicity used by the decomposition matrix is that a business process task or a data flow process is atomic if every input relates to every output in the decomposition matrix. In other words, there are check marks in every box of the matrix. Atomic tasks and processes are an important aspect of the incremental SOA analysis.

It is possible that the decomposition matrix might give you some new ideas or help you get past a sticking point in your design process. In that way, it acts much like having another designer in the room. The decomposition matrix is not a design methodology. It is meant to be a design aid. You can use it with whatever methodology you prefer since it is just another "designer" in the room.

The next section provides an example of how this tool works.

Business Process Diagram

To illustrate how the decomposition matrix works, I will use an example from a series of blog posts that start at *http://www.designdecomposition.com/blog/?p=6*. This example uses a set of inputs and outputs for a travel coordinator. Using those inputs and outputs, the decomposition matrix tool will generate a business process diagram.

The inputs and outputs in Figure 10.1 should be familiar to most people who have taken a business trip. They involve finding airline flights, a rental car, and hotel rooms for a set of travel dates along with making the reservations and obtaining driving instructions. Figure 10.1 shows this decomposition matrix.

You need to consider the relationship between only one row and one column at a time when using the decomposition matrix. These are the binary decisions mentioned earlier. For example, you could describe the relationship of the first row and first column as "the input of travel dates and locations that *occurs before or concurrently with the output* for a flight availability request."

The portion in italics is an example of the type of phrasing you should use. You may read across the row or down a column using the italicized phrasing.

Considering just one row and one column at a time makes it easier to work with larger designs. There is no need to try to keep the entire design in your head. You just need to think about each relationship one at a time.

Arranging flights involves using the travel dates and locations to request a list of available flights. Sometimes you may need to make multiple requests with different flight times or you may make requests to multiple airlines. Figure 10.1 shows this with a check mark in the second row, flight availability response, and first column, flight availability request. The third row, flight reservation response, is not checked in the first column, because you cannot have a response before a request.

The fourth column shows the inputs that occur before or concurrently with the input to a car rental reservation request. Before making a reservation request, you need to know that cars are available for your travel dates and locations. You also need to know if flights and hotel rooms are available. You do not, however, need to reserve a room before a car. On the other hand, car rental agencies often ask for a flight number at the time of rental. So there is a check mark in the third row, flight reservation response, for the fourth column. This occurs before or concurrently with the output for a car rental reservation request.

The generated business process diagram is shown in Figure 10.2. The diagram uses a subset of the business process modeling notation (BPMN).[3] The tool does not generate labels for the tasks. I have added task labels to this diagram.

There are a couple of ways the generated diagram can give you hints that there are problems with the check marks in your decomposition matrix:

This example is from the first edition of this book. The idea that a VPA—like the one in the story about C.R.'s business trip—could make all travel arrangements was not considered when I wrote the first edition. Nevertheless, making travel arrangements is an almost universally understood process so I decided it is still a useful example for the decomposition matrix.

---

[3] Business process modeling notation (BPMN), Object Management Group, *http://www.bpmn.org/*.

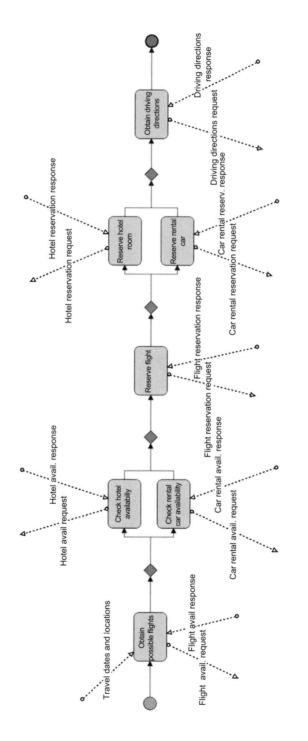

Figure 10.2 Generated business process diagram.

- If you have had trouble coming up with any of the labels, that could be a hint that the inputs and outputs might not have the correct check marks or perhaps an input or output was overlooked.
- If the diagram is confusing, that is a hint that the check marks might not be correct. An example of something confusing is a request for something coming in after its related response.

You can "play" with the inputs and outputs to see what happens to the generated diagram. This is not a complete design tool. At some point you may want to transcribe a generated diagram into your design tool, much like you would if you used a whiteboard.

Data Flow Diagram

The next example generates a Web services API or services interface layer for legacy systems. Figure 10.3 shows the decomposition matrix. The inputs are from some type of legacy system. Some of the possible outputs are also shown in the decomposition matrix. It is obviously simpler than the real world, but it serves as an illustration of how the tool can be used.

You can phrase a relationship in Figure 10.3 as "the input of invoice *is used directly or indirectly* for the output of payments." The italicized portion of the phrase

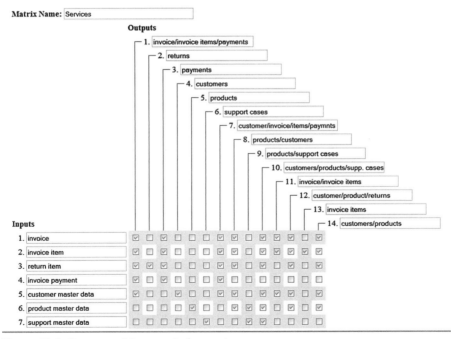

Figure 10.3 Decomposition matrix for services.

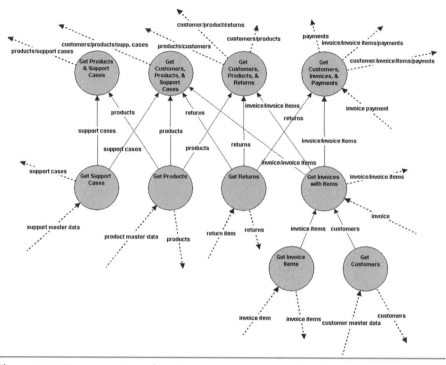

Figure 10.4 Decomposition of services.

is important. Note that this is different from how relationships are described for business process diagrams. In this case, we are dealing with data flow and not the sequencing that business process tasks require.

Figure 10.4 shows the decomposition of services based on the matrix.[4] The processes have been labeled. Just like with the business process diagrams, the tool leaves labeling up to the user. Again, if it is difficult to label a process or if the diagram is confusing, that is a hint that the inputs and outputs may not be complete or that some check marks are missing.

The top-level processes in Figure 10.4 represent the Web services API or service interface layer. Some of the top-level processes have multiple outputs. This indicates that the input parameters will need to specify the XML tags (in this case) to include in the output. Such input parameters are not shown in data flow diagrams, but they

---

[4] At the time the website was implemented, the Service Oriented Architecture Modeling Language (SoaML) notation was not available. If you wish, it is not hard to manually create an SoaML diagram from the data flow diagrams. SoaML specifications are from the Object Management Group, *http://www.omg.org/spec/SoaML/*.

will be needed when you design the services. Any data flow diagram shows only the flow of data and not the control input parameters.

The services below the top level are reusable components that have been factored out. Depending on your implementation, you could implement them as services or as library code components.

Just like with the business process decomposition, this tool allows you to "play" with inputs and outputs to see the effects. At some point, you will want to transcribe the decomposition into your design tool.

Five Principles for the Incremental SOA Analysis

The incremental SOA analysis uses these three tools in a way that improves the chances of success for a project. There are five principles that provide the basis for the incremental SOA analysis:

1. **Make projects as small as possible.** This has already been discussed in the previous chapter, but in this technique "small" has a specific meaning. Projects involve only a single atomic task in the business process diagram generated from the business process analysis. For example, each of the tasks in Figure 10.2 would be a separate project.
2. **Involve stakeholders appropriately and as much as possible.** Engaging the appropriate people was discussed in Chapter 8. The incremental SOA analysis is designed for this type of engagement.
3. **Make decisions as late as possible.** The later you can make a decision, the more likely you will have accurate or more complete information on which to make your decision.
4. **Weaken the restraining forces within the project as much as possible.** Chapter 5 introduced force field analysis and described why weakening restraining forces is often better than strengthening driving forces. By weakening restraining forces, you are increasing your chances of success.
5. **Realize that your SOA will never be done.** For most organizations, an SOA will be ever changing because it will need to respond to the changing nature of business and technology. The primary goal of this incremental SOA analysis is to eventually position your organization so that it can respond quickly to those changes. It will provide you with a loosely coupled (see page 31) architecture that should improve your organization's ability to change. A secondary goal is to leave you with functioning architecture whenever you stop. Budgets and other demands often derail the best-laid development plans. With this type of analysis, you should be able to restart your SOA development at some later time if work is suspended for some reason.

Incremental SOA Analysis

Figure 10.5 shows the process for incremental SOA analysis. The workflow shown in Figure 10.5 is my suggestion for how to implement the five principles for the incremental SOA analysis.

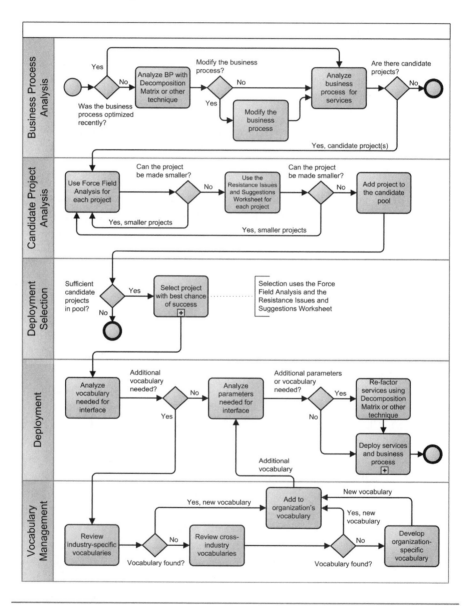

Figure 10.5 Incremental SOA analysis.

This analysis is shown as a workflow because the diagramming provides a rigor beyond a textual description. The following sections provide some notes for each of the tasks and processes in this analysis.

BUSINESS PROCESS ANALYSIS LANE

The business process analysis lane is where the analysis starts. (The workflow in Figure 10.5 is divided into five lanes—the business process analysis lane is at the top.) The purpose of the activity in this lane is to develop a small number of candidate projects that can move on to candidate project analysis described in the next lane. The intent is not to analyze all of the organization's processes. The assumption is that there are some known opportunities for improvement suitable for analysis. The three tasks in this lane are described in the following subsections.

Analyze the Business Process with Decomposition Matrix or Other Technique

If you have a preferred analysis technique, use it. If you don't, you might consider using the decomposition matrix tool described earlier in this chapter.

The decomposition matrix provides a way to think differently about the system you are about to analyze. This tool can be used to get information from the various stakeholders. Ideally, you should do this in a group setting to allow the stakeholders to share their views on the business process.

Modify the Business Process

Modify the business process until all tasks are atomic.

Analyze the Business Process for Services

Review the atomic tasks for the candidate project. Restricting work to an atomic task is part of the principle of making projects as small as possible. A candidate project should:

- **Be noticeably different.** The point here is to avoid just replacing something that most people don't really see. For example, you could use Web services to replace an in-house communication protocol. There is nothing wrong with that. It just may not impress too many people with the power of SOA. What might impress people is using the connection capability of Web services to combine internal information with something from the cloud so that a business process is enhanced or made simpler.

- **Be the only project you do for now.** What if you only had time and money to do one SOA-related project? That is consistent with the principle that your SOA is never done but that you can build it incrementally as time and money permits. So, pick something that is useful without needing a follow-up project.

CANDIDATE PROJECT ANALYSIS LANE

The candidate project analysis lane analyzes the candidate project using force field analysis along with the resistance issues and suggestions worksheets. This lane adds an approach that might allow you to make projects even smaller.

Use Force Field Analysis for Each Project

As mentioned in Chapter 5, force field analysis uncovers the driving and restraining forces for the desired change related to the candidate project. You can get a group involved with the visual nature of force field analysis using flip charts or a whiteboard. Having a group inspect the completed force field analysis may allow you to discover that a project can be made smaller. For example, you may find that a restraining force is the lack of a tool to develop the service interface. You could decide that experimenting with development tools is a project unto itself. Therefore, the candidate project could be divided into two projects. One project is tool experimentation and selection. By dividing the candidate project into two projects, you eliminate a restraining force on the original candidate project and you get two smaller projects—one that is only tool selection. Presumably, the selected tool will also be used in future projects.

Use the Resistance Issues and Suggestions Worksheet for Each Project

The worksheet for resistance issues and suggestions (see page 102) lists the restraining forces found in the force field analysis and provides space for entering the suggested ways to address each restraining force. As with force field analysis, inspecting the completed worksheet may allow you to discover a way to make a project smaller. For example, one restraining force might be the lack of experience with Web services and another might be unfamiliarity with XML. The suggestions in the worksheet to address both restraining forces might be a combined XML and Web services course. That course could be a separate project. The original project could be divided into two projects. In this way, you eliminate two restraining forces on the original candidate project and you get a smaller project. In this case, the smaller project is training.

Add the Project to the Candidate Pool

If force field analysis and the resistance issues and suggestions worksheet cannot make the candidate project smaller, then that project can be added to the candidate pool. You should have at least a few projects in the pool before selecting a project for deployment.

DEPLOYMENT SELECTION LANE

The deployment selection lane selects the project for deployment. Only one process appears in this lane, but for a given organization there could be more processes or tasks based on the organization's project selection criteria. For example, some type of financial justification might need to be added at this point as a factor to be considered in project selection.

SELECT A PROJECT WITH THE BEST CHANCE OF SUCCESS

Following the principles of this analysis, pick the project with the shortest duration. It will most likely be the one with the greatest chance of success. The duration of the project is based on the estimation technique your organization uses, and the chance of success is determined based on inspection of the final force field analysis and worksheet for resistance issues and suggestions. Of course, these forces sometimes can be difficult to quantify. Nevertheless, the force field analysis and worksheet provide a way to inform you whether one project versus another project is more likely to succeed.

Note that there is a "+" at the base of this process in Figure 10.5. That indicates that there are subprocesses. Since these subprocesses can vary by organization, the details are not shown in the figure.

DEPLOYMENT LANE

This lane has the workflow for deployment. Notice that decisions on vocabulary and interface parameters have been deferred until this time in keeping with the principle of making decisions as late as possible.

Analyze Vocabulary Needed for Interface

You might not have expected that the semantic vocabulary needs are deferred until this point. In reality, the semantic vocabulary needed is not a factor until this point. If additional vocabulary is needed, the workflow will move to the vocabulary management lane.

Analyze Parameters Needed for Interface

Here you need to determine the parameters required for the service interface. If there is a change in vocabulary or parameters, then it will be necessary to consider refactoring services.

Refactor Services Using Decomposition Matrix or Other Technique

If there is a need for additional vocabulary or parameters for the interface, then there is a possibility that the services may need to be refactored. The refactoring of services is part of deployment to keep the project self-contained and complete at the end of deployment. This adheres to the principle where you need to assume your SOA may never be done. You want to be at a reasonable stopping point of completion at the end of every project. Refactoring ensures that the services are at the right level of service granularity at the end of each project.

The refactoring of services suggests using the decomposition matrix or using a technique of your choice to refactor services. If you use the decomposition matrix, the website will generate diagrams with processes that can be either services or internal functions. Each process will be factored at an atomic level. Those processes that have interfaces with the business processes will be part of a service interface. The processes that do not interface with business processes will most likely be implemented as a function. Of course, you may find yourself refactoring functions into services based on the needs of that future project. Nevertheless, you should not anticipate refactoring. The next project or projects may not require refactoring. This way, you have just as many services needed right now as opposed to creating additional services in anticipation of future needs. Besides, you might guess wrong on the factoring of future services.

Deploy Services and Business Processes

The deployment of services and business processes is shown as a process in the model because organizations will have multiple tasks related to deployment. The model ends after deployment. At this point, the system should be at a stable state with new and or updated services, a semantic vocabulary sufficient for the services, and all services at the right level of granularity.

Note that there is a "+" at the base of this process in Figure 10.5. That indicates that there are subprocesses. Since these subprocesses can vary by organization, the details are not shown in the figure.

VOCABULARY MANAGEMENT LANE

The vocabulary management lane supports the deployment lane in cases where additional semantic vocabulary is needed.

Review Industry-Specific Vocabularies

No one should develop a new semantic vocabulary if it can be avoided. Developing a vocabulary can become a black hole from which you may not return. In many organizations, it is easy to find differing definitions of such common terms as *serial number* or *account*. It is equally easy to find differing terms that have the same definition. Arguing over who is right can be never ending.

The increasing global reach of even the smallest of organizations means that it is probably more important to use vocabulary terms and meanings consistent with the rest of the world rather than consistent within an organization. This is one reason industry groups developed standard semantic vocabularies. It is best to adopt that part of the industry vocabulary that is needed for the project's service interface. There is a partial list of industry vocabularies on page 179. You can also use a search engine to find semantic vocabularies that apply to your industry.

Review Cross-Industry Vocabularies

If you cannot find a vocabulary designed specifically for your organization, then you should look to cross-industry vocabularies. A good place to start is the Universal Business Language (UBL), which is an OASIS standard (http://ubl.xml.org).

Develop Organization-Specific Vocabulary

As a last resort, develop an organization-specific vocabulary. If you find this necessary, develop only what is needed when it is needed. As mentioned before, this effort can easily become a black hole.

Add to the Organization's Semantic Vocabulary

In whatever way you determine additions to the semantic vocabulary, add only what is needed when it is needed. This is in keeping with the principle of making decisions as late as possible. It also reduces the number of vocabulary decisions to only those needed to support the current project, thus keeping the project duration and complexity to a minimum.

Summary

This chapter showed how to coordinate the use of three tools to help in managing change: force field analysis, the worksheet for resistance issues and suggestions, and the decomposition matrix. Using these tools can engage people in such a way that they might come to their own resolutions on technical and human change issues. Finally, this chapter showed how to integrate these tools in an incremental SOA analysis with the aim of reducing project size and increasing the chances of project success.

Getting Started with Web Services, Service-Oriented Architectures, and Cloud Computing

In this part of the book, the focus shifts to getting started with Web services, service-oriented architectures, and cloud computing. Chapter 11 provides three basic experiments that use Web services and then uses the story about C. R.'s business trip to address more advanced uses of Web services. It ends with a vision of what Web services might mean for the future. Chapter 12 provides design concepts and considerations along with staffing and change issues to take into account when establishing a service-oriented architecture. It illustrates how properly designed service interfaces can make it easier for an organization to respond to the chaos of modern business. It ends with discussion of governance. Governance is important given the likely expansion of services within an organization and the growing use of services external to an organization. Chapter 13 discusses a way to evaluate external services and the systems and hardware that support those services. Chapter 14 summarizes the Web services, service-oriented architectures, and cloud computing related to the business trip described in Chapters 1 and 2.

Getting Started with Web Services

Contents

This chapter provides an approach to getting started with Web services. It provides three basic experiments that use Web services and then uses the story about C. R.'s business trip to address more advanced uses of Web services. At the end is a vision of what Web services might mean for the future.

All Web Services Connections Look the Same

By now, you probably have noticed that the Web services protocols for connecting internal services are no different than the protocols needed for connecting internal services to external services. Web services and the pervasiveness of HTTP connections make it relatively easy to connect internal and external services together.

The Impact of Web Services

For many companies, the initial impact that Web services will have is to make existing forms of integration simpler. This will create more opportunities for integration and data exchange. These opportunities may occur within an organization or between organizations.

The story of C. R.'s business trip illustrates some examples of what Web services (along with service-oriented architecture and cloud computing) might mean for all of us. In addition to connectivity, we are seeing businesses provide all sorts of services that can be integrated[1] with internal systems. (This is the blurring of internal and external services mentioned on page 37.) Advances in technology can take advantage of these services and will eventually be able do to such things as handle travel arrangements and help us manage our lives (as illustrated by the virtual personal assistant in the story of C. R.'s business trip).

The integration opportunities presented by Web services are making the use of Web services a requirement for many organizations. The software affected will range from desktop systems and mobile devices to distributed enterprise systems and sophisticated cloud-based systems.

---

[1] With Web services, it is sometimes difficult to come up with the correct descriptive phrases. *Integrated* is not exactly the best term because the services are provided in a seamless way at many locations on the Internet. Another term often used is *mashup*, but that term does not give the sense that there is an architecture. For the purposes of this book, I use *integrated*.

Use of Web Services will Likely Spur Innovation

The problem with predicting how Web services will affect our systems is that the effect is not always immediately apparent. In some ways, it's fair to compare the evolution of the use of Web services to the evolution of the use of the Internet in how it affects all that we do. For example, when the Internet first became available, who knew that online shopping would be setting records,[2] that we would connect with friends and acquaintances via social networks, that the Internet would make it possible to stream movies and video to our desktop or TV, or that grandparents would buy personal computers to exchange email or video chat with their grandchildren? Web services constitute a similar situation in that businesses will think of all sorts of new and creative ways to use this capability.

Another way to look at C.R.'s business trip is the importance of the Internet/ cloud and the services offered. The prevalence of connections in the cloud is enticing developers to leverage those services into all sorts of new creative services that, in turn, make adoption of a service-oriented architecture (SOA) an offer few businesses can afford to refuse.

Start by Experimenting with Web Services

One way to get started with Web services is to consider small projects that have a high chance of success. Keeping the use of Web services to something basic further enhances the chance of success. Choose a project that will be helpful but not vital. Choose team members who like to play with possibilities. Be sure to communicate that the project is an experiment.

USE AN EXTERNAL SERVICE

Probably the best place to start is using an external service. There are many simple external services from which to choose. For example, you could use weather forecasts, stock information, or news feeds. More examples of relatively simple external services can be found at *http://www.programmableweb.com/apis/ directory.*

---

[2] "Holiday Shoppers Flocking Online Create Record Breaking Sales," *http://www.forbes.com/sites/ anthonydemarco/2011/11/27/holiday-shoppers-flocking-online-create-record-breaking-sales/.*

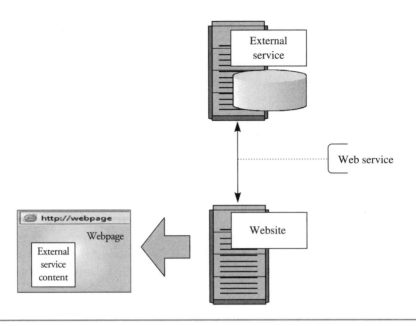

Figure 11.1 Using an external service to display content on a webpage.

Perhaps the easiest project is to create a webpage that displays something available from an external service. This project would provide experience at using Web services for sending and receiving messages. It will give you an idea of how Web services work and where you might want to try your hand at developing an internal service. Figure 11.1 illustrates using an external service to display content on a webpage.

DEVELOP AN INTERNAL SERVICE

Experimenting with the development of an internal service allows your organization to get more deeply into the details of Web services. There are two options for developing an internal service:

■ Develop an entirely new service.
■ Develop a service that uses an existing system.

If you have existing systems that you would like to use with Web services, the second option might be more useful.

This project is similar to the previous one. The difference is that the content displayed comes from an internal system. Examples of such access include obtaining customer contact information or internal employee telephone numbers.

This requires the development of an adapter. It will do two things:

1. Transform a Web services message into a request format that can be accepted by the internal system.
2. Transform the response from the internal system into a Web services message.

There are adapter toolkits to help you build an adapter. Of course, if your organization is more likely to use existing adapters, consider either an open-source adapter or a commercial adapter for an existing system and incorporate that adapter into this project. Figure 11.2 illustrates using an internal service to display content on a webpage.

EXCHANGE DATA BETWEEN EXISTING SYSTEMS

If your organization is likely to use Web services to exchange data between existing internal systems, then it would be appropriate to add an experimental project

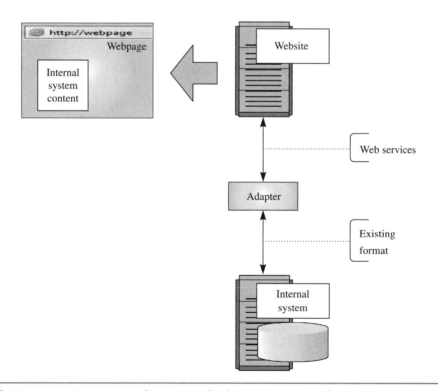

Figure 11.2 Using an internal service to display content on a webpage.

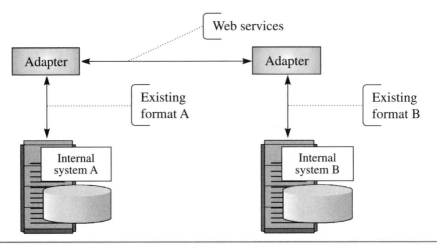

Figure 11.3 Using Web services to exchange data between internal systems.

that does just that. Figure 11.3 illustrates this exchange of data between internal systems.

This project uses the experience from the previous experimental project of using an adapter. In this project, however, two internal systems exchange data. For example, both systems A and B may allow users to enter customer address and contact information. If one system updates this customer information, the other system should also receive the update. Another example might be that system A has the master account for customer information and system B may request system A to validate that a customer identification number is correct.

Both systems A and B would need adapters. The development would require agreement on the semantics of the vocabulary in the messages exchanged by the adapters. This would create the opportunity to investigate and possibly use the semantic vocabulary developed by standards efforts in your industry.

USE AN ESB

Many organizations are also likely to use an enterprise service bus (ESB). If your organization is planning to use an ESB, then the previous experiment can be modified to include one. Figure 11.4 shows the use of Web services with an ESB to exchange data between internal systems.

The intent of this experimental project is to gain appreciation of the issues related to message routing as well as experience in using an ESB. You probably won't need to buy an ESB for this experiment. There are open-source ESBs, some vendors may let you try their ESBs, and—perhaps even simpler—some ESBs are available as a service in the cloud.

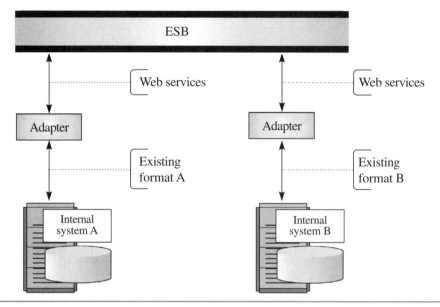

Figure 11.4 Using Web services with an ESB to exchange data between internal systems.

STAFFING ISSUES

It is important to pick the right people to do this experimentation. Frankly, in most situations it is risky to involve people who have never expressed much interest in trying something new. Instead, choose people who like to experiment and take risks. For many organizations, it would be good to bring in someone from outside the organization who is familiar with Web services to mentor developers during these efforts. The mentor would be a "second set of eyes" during this experimentation stage and would be a great source of information. Keep the project team small. A few people would be appropriate for most organizations.

LIKELY CHANGE ISSUES

The most likely change issues you will encounter are:

- **Lack of training/understanding.** This is a rational concern. People will need training on Web services. You will need to find the appropriate training for those involved in the experimentation. Also, you need to be ready to dispel any misunderstandings concerning the use of Web services by your organization.
- **Inertia—why change?** Be prepared to communicate on many levels and in many ways why you want this experimentation to occur. Be available for personal chats. Be prepared, as well, to really listen to concerns expressed.

Adapt Existing Systems to Use Web Services

Once you have some experience using Web services, look for some places in your existing systems where Web services could save time and money in the short term. At this point, you might consider trying the incremental SOA analysis introduced in Chapter 10. It might help you ensure that you are taking on the smallest, shortest-duration project.

To illustrate adapting existing systems to Web services, I'm going to return to the story about C.R. His organization had a repository that was originally an enterprise data warehouse (EDW). Like many organizations, C.R.'s had common data that was replicated in multiple systems, creating an opportunity. For example, his organization had common customer data in multiple systems. These systems were either developed over time in separate departments or they were purchased software packages. Some were systems used by other organizations that his organization had acquired over time. In any case, the systems were different, had replicated data, and in some cases, inconsistent data. C.R.'s organization saw business advantages to creating more visibility of customers for such purposes as cross-selling among departments, creating new packages of products for specific customers, and simply reducing waste in misrouted or duplicated mail.

Enterprise Database Warehouse

For some people, the very idea of creating an EDW can be discouraging. Many of us have had the experience of failed efforts to create master files like an EDW (see page 100). Here are some tips:

- **Use an existing master file.** You might already have a master file that is part of packaged software your organization owns. It might make sense to adopt that as the master file. If you do not have a master file in packaged software your organization owns but are considering the purchase of packaged software, check to see if the software being considered includes a master file that could be used as an EDW.
- **Buy a model.** This option is often overlooked. Many models can be purchased. Sometimes they are referred to as universal data models (see page 108). The fact is that, although every organization is unique in some way, most of the data is pretty standard. For example, there are practical and flexible models for keeping basic customer information such as addresses and other contact information. Often, these models are simply better than anything an organization might build itself. Experienced modelers who have created models for many organizations usually are the people who design these models. If you buy a model, you should resist any efforts to extensively modify it. See the next tip.
- **Don't start a modeling project.** A modeling project opens your organization to any number of restraining forces, including our problems are special, power of an

internal expert, and lack of training and understanding. The lack of training and understanding is significant. Data modeling appears deceptively simple until you get into it. Even if you are doing something as basic as a customer master, you can get yourself pretty knotted up in the options of data modeling. A modeling project also is an opportunity to add "bells and whistles" to a basic model. Starting a modeling project is essentially creating an environment for "analysis paralysis."

■ **Start small.** Your EDW does not need to be perfect. It simply needs to be useful or effective. Also, you can always add to your EDW at some later date. So, if either an existing master file or a purchased model has many fields you could populate, try to limit the data to what might be most useful. Don't make the project any larger than it needs to be. You can always add more data to the EDW later.

C. R.'s organization took on the task of data cleansing to populate the EDW. Figure 11.5 illustrates this. An EDW is at the left in the figure. At the right is an existing internal system, and existing applications are above the existing system.

Creating an EDW is a good time to make sure the data you are using is the best possible. This process is often called data cleansing. Data cleansing can become a large project in itself, depending on the existing system and the number of existing systems that will be used for the customer master. You might consider purchasing an extract, transform, and load (ETL) software product if you expect to use many existing systems that will require significant data cleansing.

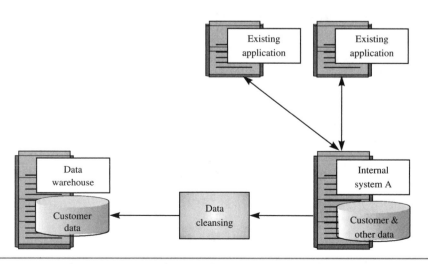

Figure 11.5 Creating a customer data warehouse.

It may seem that I have oversimplified what needs to be done. In a sense I have, but only because at this point the EDW is meant to achieve a limited goal of consolidating a small amount of data—in this example, customer master data. In C. R.'s story, the EDW did eventually grow to be very large. C. R.'s organization, like most organizations, had multiple sources of customer data in its existing systems. This process started with one existing system and then moved on to others.

CONNECT COMPONENTS TO WEB SERVICES

Figure 11.6 shows the three components that C. R.'s organization connected using Web services:

- ESB
- EDW that was populated after data cleansing along with associated business intelligence (BI)/analytics software
- Existing system using a Web services adapter

C. R.'s organization decided that to keep the EDW updated, changes were needed to internal system A in Figure 11.6. Internal system A needed to send updates to the EDW as they came in from the existing applications. Those updates were routed to the data warehouse using the ESB. Internal system A was also updated so that the data going to the data warehouse was of the highest quality.

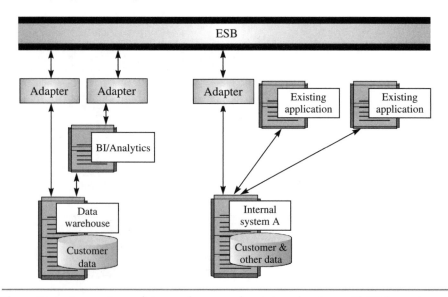

Figure 11.6 Connecting a data warehouse and an internal system with Web services.

ADDITIONAL SYSTEMS

C. R.'s organization repeated the data cleansing and populating of the EDW for each of their additional systems that would provide data for the EDW. Eventually, the systems architecture looked like Figure 11.7.

With the data from the additional systems, the EDW is the source of data for the development of future services. That reduced the impact on the existing internal operational systems.

> For some organizations, this might be an intensive process if there are inconsistencies among the data sources. Sometimes these inconsistencies will not be able to be resolved using programming. For example, if the same customer has two different addresses, it will be necessary for a person to determine if the addresses should be the same or if they represent two different locations of the same customer.

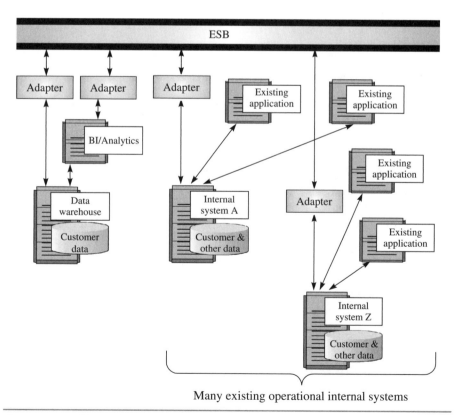

Figure 11.7 Adding additional systems.

In summary, for C. R.'s organization, the EDW and ESB:

- Reduced the risk of any one internal system not being able to complete processing that is dependent on data from another system.
- Required using fewer adapters since each internal system needs only to have an adapter that works with the ESB.
- Reduced the possible negative impact of requests for data that is outside the normal processing of the internal systems.

Staffing Issues

For this type of effort, costs could start to increase significantly because more people are getting involved. At this point, you could have at least one person but perhaps two or three people who have a reasonable understanding of Web services. They can form the core of this team along with a few new people. The entire team, however, should be under seven people. This is also a good time to establish the methodology that will be used going forward.

Likely Change Issues

The most likely change issues you will encounter in this type effort are:

- **Lack of training/understanding.** This is still a rational concern. The new people will likely need training. Don't assume that the people who have been doing the experimentation are the right ones to do the training. It would be best to have the training done professionally so that any bad habits that may have crept in aren't passed along. Also, be ready to dispel any misunderstandings concerning Web services and SOAs. This will likely require communication in many ways on many levels, including upper management.
- **Power of the internal "expert."** Be careful that an internal expert does not sink the project in this stage. It is important that you select the right people and plan for a second set of eyes for each person involved. This may help counter the internal expert if he or she is on the team.
- **Our problems are special.** This will show up if you buy a model. It will be important to get this resistance out in the open as soon as possible so that you can deal with it. Recall the "But it's so complicated!" scenario on page 95. It could happen to you.

Vision of the Future

The effect of Web services means we are going to have fewer people involved in IT. The jobs in IT will also generally change to creating architectures and often realizing those architectures by making the connections to services in the cloud. At the same time, the quality of software will improve because progressively less new code will need to be written.

The industry will standardize on the capabilities of various services. An analogy was provided earlier to how the audio-video (AV) industry eventually settled on the capabilities of various AV components. The same will happen with services. As this happens, it will become easier to find services in the cloud and connect them with internal services. Already, fewer people build custom software because it is cheaper to purchase commercial off-the-shelf software and tailor it to an organization's needs. This is a trend that will continue with services. For many organizations, staying competitive will mean taking advantage of the services available in the cloud. Some organizations may find that they have unique services that they can provide, and IT staff will be needed to create those services. Nevertheless, there will be fewer jobs involving custom development.

With the eventual standardization of services, it will become easier to replace one service with another. (This would be similar to replacing one AV receiver component with another that has more capabilities.) This should be a clarion call to service providers to protect the quality of their product. There will be fewer reasons for organizations to put up with inferior software if it is easy to swap in a service from a different vendor.

Summary

This chapter provided an approach to getting started with Web services with three basic experiments meant to create a familiarity with using Web services. Following that, the chapter used the story about C.R.'s business trip to address more advanced uses of Web services. A vision of what Web services might mean for the future was provided at the end.

Although it might have looked like it, this chapter did not address SOA. Chapter 12 provides suggestions for getting started with SOAs.

Chapter 12

Getting Started with Service-Oriented Architectures

Contents

A major advantage of using a service-oriented architecture (SOA) with Web services is that it fits in with the general chaos of business. There are many forces contributing to this chaos: organizations are acquired and divested, organizations restructure themselves, new products need to be sold, competition forces quick responses, and, of course, there's more and it is ever changing.

Historically, it has been a struggle for IT groups to respond to this business chaos. An SOA provides a way to be more nimble in the responses. If an SOA is designed properly, it will approach the type of plug-compatibility that I have been alluding to with the audio-video (AV) examples sprinkled throughout this book.

Nevertheless, just using Web services for making connections does not guarantee your organization will have a functional SOA. The trick is in how you design your SOA.

This chapter provides design concepts and considerations along with staffing and change issues to take into account when establishing an SOA. It illustrates how a properly designed service interface can make it easier for an organization to respond to the chaos of modern business. At the end, there is a discussion of SOA governance.

▌ Establish a Service-Oriented Architecture

I have waited until this point before suggesting that you establish an architecture, because it is important to have the experiences experimenting with Web services described in Chapter 11. An architecture based on experience is much more likely to succeed than one that is based on just reading a book or thinking about the technology.

Anchor an SOA in what your organization really needs and what your people are capable of accomplishing. Recall from Chapter 9 that smaller projects are more focused and are more likely to succeed. Large projects are likely to fail. Since 1994, the Standish Group has conducted studies on IT development projects, compiling the results in the *Chaos Reports*. In 2005, Watts S. Humphrey of the Software Engineering Institute looked at the Standish Group's data by project size. His research showed that half of the smaller projects succeeded, whereas none of the largest projects did.[1]

You may want to go back to Chapter 10 to review the approach to developing an SOA as a series of small incremental projects.

DESIGN CONSIDERATIONS

1. **Adopt industry standards.** These standards include Web services and industry-standard semantic vocabularies. (The industry group specifying the standard semantic vocabularies could also be identified. See page 179 for a sample of vocabularies by industry.)

---

[1] Watts S. Humphrey "Why Big Software Projects Fail: The 12 Key Questions." *CrossTalk: The Journal of Defense Software Engineering,* March 2005.

2. **Use commercial off-the-shelf software as much as possible.** The software must provide Web services adapters.

3. **Encapsulate legacy applications with interfaces that meet industry standards.** Web services must be used for the interface.

4. **Use a data-independent layer between applications and data to hide the structure of the underlying data.** All interaction must be through Web services.

5. **Design services for reusability.** Chapter 10 suggests one technique for determining the right "size" or granularity of a service. Use some type of methodology to improve the chances that the services are reusable.

6. **Every service must be able to receive messages multiple times with no adverse effects.** For example, assume a service can receive updates to customer data. That service must be able to receive the same update more than once without affecting the data. The reason for this is that the sending service may, for various reasons, send data multiple times. This can happen when a system comes up after being down for a period of time. It may have some type of checkpoint that is taken after some multiple of messages go out. If the system goes down between checkpoints, some messages may need to be sent again to be sure they went out. It can also happen through mistakes in programming, multiple data requests, or simply unforeseen actions.

7. **Track and manage the use of services.** If people see services as useful, they are going to be used—perhaps in new and unusual ways (which often may be a good thing). It is important to consider tracking the use of services. Amazon Web Services (AWS) provides a model to consider:

   ■ **Unique token.** Each developer has a unique token in AWS that is used to track usage, payments, and so on.

   ■ **Versioning.** The incoming messages to AWS specify the version of the messaging and XML vocabulary to use. This allows changing the messaging in the AWS without requiring all users to also make changes. Only users interested in the change are affected.

   ■ **Response groups.** The incoming messages to AWS specify the desired response groups. Each response group contains certain data. This is an option to consider since, like the decomposition of services shown in Figure 10.4, it is possible to have services returning multiple types of responses. This could be achieved using response groups. This is extra work but with benefits. It provides increased flexibility for enhancing service responses and allows for tracking usage.

8. **High-volume, high-speed messages should be sent within a service and low-volume, low-speed messages should be sent between services.** This is one of those "relative" design considerations. Web services, no matter what, are going to run significantly slower than communication within most internal systems.

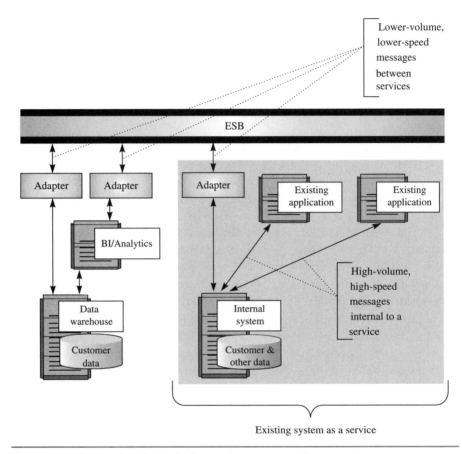

Figure 12.1 Keep high-volume, high-speed messages within a service.

Try to keep the high-volume, high-speed messages within a service. Figure 12.1 illustrates keeping high-volume, high-speed messages within an internal system that is also being used as a service.

9. **Balance the conflict between indeterminate and operational access.** This conflict is often quite apparent when using an existing system as a service. That existing system was not necessarily designed for indeterminate or erratic requests. Having to deal with those requests with the service responsiveness expected is sometimes difficult to do with an existing system. Figure 12.2 illustrates this issue. (This issue is explored more later in this chapter.)

STAFFING ISSUES

By now you should have an effective team of seven or fewer people who are very capable of taking on short-term projects. Your methodology should also be well established.

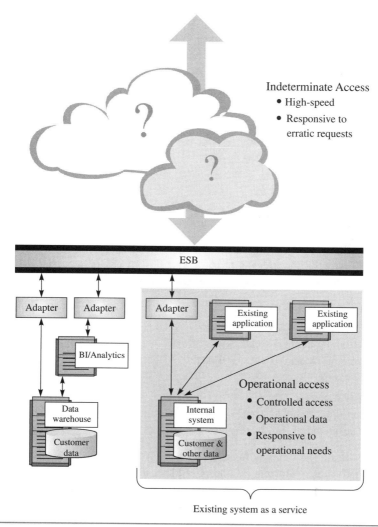

Figure 12.2 Conflict between indeterminate and operational access.

LIKELY CHANGE ISSUES

The most likely change issues you will encounter at this stage are:

- **Feeling that jobs may be threatened.** The you know what will really hit the fan at this stage. For many organizations, it will be obvious that the size of the IT staff will begin to decrease and jobs might genuinely be threatened. Be prepared to communicate openly about this as soon as possible so that people have time to make decisions.

■ **Not invented here.** You are likely to be considering external services at this stage. It is very human to resist this. Be sure to get this resistance out in the open and really listen to concerns to make sure any legitimate concerns are addressed.

■ **Our problems are special.** This relates to the feeling that jobs may be threatened. Be sure to get these concerns out in the open to see if there is any real concern that the special issues are being overlooked. Chances are very likely that the problems are not special. Be prepared to communicate this effectively. Be sure to keep management informed as the word spreads through the grapevine that "special issues" are being overlooked.

What If Things Are Not Going as Planned?

The example development illustrated in Figure 11.7 addressed the design-related restraining forces for adopting an SOA. Those design issues appeared in the force field analysis illustrated by Figure 6.9 and are as follows:

■ Deciding what data to route
■ Delays getting data updates distributed
■ Deciding what data to warehouse
■ Delays in getting data to the warehouse
■ Redundancy of data
■ Data quality issues
■ Effects on operational systems for up-to-the-moment data requests
■ Identification and design of services

But what if things are not going as planned? I'll go back to the story about C. R.'s organization to illustrate problems and possible responses.

Figure 12.3 represents, at one point, the systems supporting the SOA for C. R.'s organization (Figure 11.7 is essentially a subset of this figure). To add more detail to the story, let's say two issues appeared at this point in the use of the SOA:

1. The data warehouse was growing much faster than expected.
2. The response time of the services provided by an internal system was inadequate and the indeterminate access requests were adversely impacting the operational system. This is the issue illustrated by Figure 12.2.

THE DATA WAREHOUSE WAS GROWING MUCH FASTER THAN EXPECTED

The response to the first issue was described in the section on adopting a platform as a service (PaaS) starting on page 74. This described how C. R.'s organization moved to a virtual private cloud to provide for a big data store, and is illustrated by Figure 12.4.

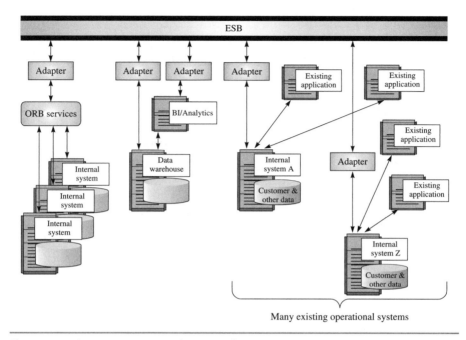

Figure 12.3 Systems supporting the SOA of C. R.'s organization.

The PaaS includes tools to help develop, manage, and analyze the data in big data stores. It provides an ESB within the virtual private cloud that is optimized for the big data store and the business intelligence (BI)/analytics software.

The Internet is represented by the horizontal shaded area. Web services are shown as a black line within the shaded area. This represents that Web services protocols (SOAP, REST, JSON, etc.) are a subset of the protocols that can be used on the Internet.

Note the adapters aligned with the big data and BI/analytics in the virtual private cloud. They are needed because those services use a somewhat different semantic vocabulary than the one used by C. R.'s organization.

THE RESPONSE TIME OF THE SERVICES PROVIDED BY AN INTERNAL SYSTEM WAS INADEQUATE

The second issue can be problematic. C. R.'s organization, like many others, was not in a position to change the internal system that was being adversely affected when used as a service. One solution is a middle-tier architecture that uses persistent caching.

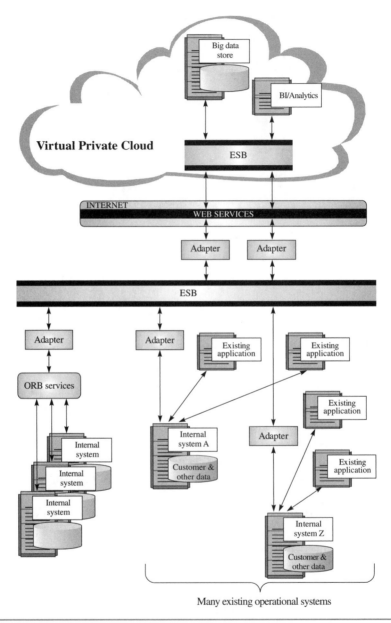

Figure 12.4 Using a PaaS cloud provider for a big data store and BI/analytics.

This section goes into some technical detail. The purpose is to show that the systems underlying a service can go through significant changes, and yet the services themselves are affected very little.

Basics of a Middle-Tier Architecture

A middle-tier architecture is one way to leverage the use of existing systems and databases. The middle tier changes where integration occurs. Instead of directly integrating existing systems and databases, a new layer is developed so that the integration occurs in the middle tier. Moving integration to the middle tier is the solution used by C.R.'s organization to address the conflict between indeterminate and operational access.

Figure 12.5 illustrates the basics of a middle-tier architecture[2] that uses an application server and a middle-tier database. The middle tier is above internal systems. One of the internal systems that we have covered so far is at the bottom of the figure. It is also used as a service.

Note that the adapter is at the bottom of the middle tier, above the internal system as it was in Figure 12.4. Since this application server is presumably new development, it can use the same semantic vocabulary and Web services message format as the ESB. An adapter is not needed for the application server.

Persistence in the Middle Tier

It is possible to add persistence to the middle tier. Adding persistence to the middle tier makes sense in situations that either have too much data to keep in the application server cache or situations where you need the protection of persistence to make sure no data would be lost before it can be written to the internal system. It can also be a way to boost performance of services provided by an application server when it needs to access data. Middle-tier persistence, however, will require additional development.

A persistent cache adds capabilities to the in-memory cache. These include:

- Expanded caching
- Protected caching
- Caching performance gain

---

[2]There are various terms for the tiers in systems architecture. For this discussion, *middle tier* is used because it is in the middle between user systems and the internal system.

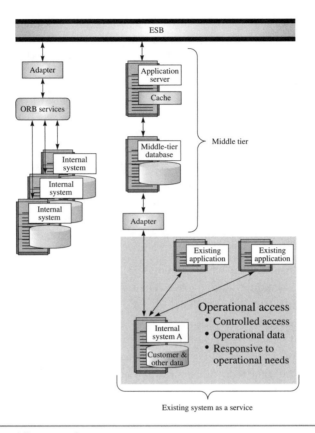

Figure 12.5 Middle-tier architecture.

The examples assume that a database will be used in the middle tier to provide the persistent cache. A database manager ensures that all transactions will be recorded properly and has recovery and backup capabilities, if needed.

Expanded Caching

There are several ways that a cache could be populated:

1. **On an as-needed basis.** An instance moves into the cache only when a program requests to read the values of the instance.
2. **Fully populated at start time.** All instances needed in the cache are populated when the system starts up.
3. **A combination of the first two.** An example is populating the cache with the most likely instances that are needed and then moving additional instances into the cache when a program requests to read the values of the instances.

In any of these cases, the cache size simply could be too large to efficiently keep in memory. A middle-tier database could act as an expanded cache to offload some of the data cached in memory.

Using a middle-tier database as an expanded cache adds options when the underlying internal system is updated. The updates could occur as they happen or at intervals, depending on the needs of the organization. For example, one option would be to populate the middle-tier database from the internal system at the beginning of a business day. All updates could be kept in the middle-tier database. These updates could then be written to the internal system at the end of the day or at intervals during the day.

Protected Caching

If all middle-tier cache updates are written to a middle-tier database, then the cached updates are not lost if the application server should fail. They can be recovered from the middle-tier database when the application server is restored. This, of course, would not be necessary if updates to the internal system are made every time an update occurs. That, however, can create a performance hit to the middle tier, as will be discussed in the next section.

Caching Performance Gain

If the middle-tier database uses the same data model as the middle-tier cache, there is a good chance that performance will be significantly better than if updates were written to the internal system as they happened.

This performance gain is possible assuming:

- The internal system uses a data structure that is different from what is needed for the service. Chances are that this is true if the internal system has been around for a while.
- The application server uses a cache that matches the needs of the object program in the application server. This cache could use either an object, XML, or other NoSQL data structure.
- The middle-tier database uses the same data model as the cache.

Given these assumptions, the time it takes to write an update to the internal system will most likely take longer than writing to the middle-tier database. As the complexity of the model used by the object program in the application server increases, the difference in the time it takes to write the update to the middle-tier database versus the internal system increases. This is because the mapping complexity also increases between the data model in the cache and the model in the internal system. The mapping simply takes time and costs performance.[3]

---

[3] More on mapping issues can be found at *http://www.service-architecture.com/object-relational-mapping/articles/mapping_layer.html*.

As a result, an update to a middle-tier database can be significantly faster and allow processing to resume much sooner than if the update was to the internal system directly.[4] Figure 12.6 shows the sequence of this processing.

Middle-Tier Databases

There are many database options available for middle-tier persistence, because middle-tier databases essentially store temporary data. This is in contrast to internal

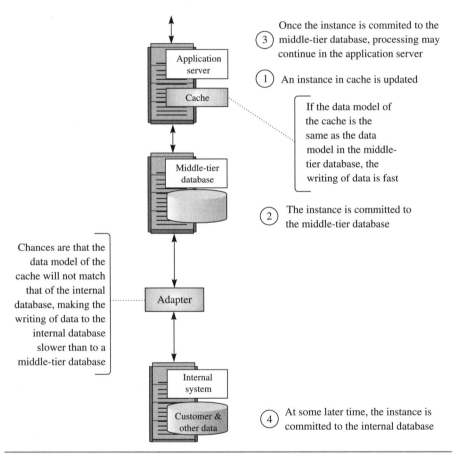

Figure 12.6 Using a persistent cache in the middle tier.

---

[4] IBM published a benchmark that showed significant performance gains with a middle-tier database between the WebSphere application server and DB2. See *http://www.service-architecture.com/application-servers/ articles/benchmark_using_a_transaction_accelerator.html*. The full benchmark paper is available from a link on that page.

system databases that are often seen as databases of record, which are expected to last "forever." When you are considering a database product for an internal system, it is reasonable to choose a database management product from a well-known, established vendor.

In contrast, middle-tier databases—because they are temporary—open up the possibilities of using technologies that might significantly improve performance and reduce development as well as maintenance costs.

There are many issues to consider in selecting a middle-tier database. A discussion of those issues goes beyond the scope of this book. More information on middle-tier persistence can be found at *http://www.service-architecture.com/object-oriented-databases/articles/middle_tier_architecture.html.*

PUTTING IT ALL TOGETHER

Figure 12.7 shows the systems supporting the SOA for C.R.'s organization after addressing the two issues that appeared after developing the enterprise data warehouse (EDW) and using an internal system as a service. The customer relationship management (CRM) from a software as a service (SaaS) cloud provider was also added for completeness.

Services and Service-Oriented Architectures

In Chapter 3, a service was described as software and hardware—and that one or more services support or automate a business function. Much of this book has focused on the software and hardware systems that are needed to support services. Let's now focus on services. Chapter 10 had a generated decomposition of services illustrated in Figure 10.4. A portion from the lower right corner of that services decomposition is shown in Figure 12.8.

Figure 12.8 represents two low-level data services. For discussion's sake, let's say these two services were part of the data services for the prior discussion of the two issues facing C.R.'s organization. The Get Customers service could relate to the data warehouse that was moved to a big data store in a PaaS cloud provider, and the Get Invoice Items could relate to the middle-tier architecture used to relieve an internal system that was adversely affected by indeterminate access because it was also used as a service.

Something had to change related to these services when the underlying systems were changed. The adapters may have needed to be changed or perhaps some code in these services needed to be changed.

Note that before these solutions were implemented, C.R.'s organization had implemented services for the data warehouse and the internal system. The important point is that only the code in low-level data services or other code below the low-level

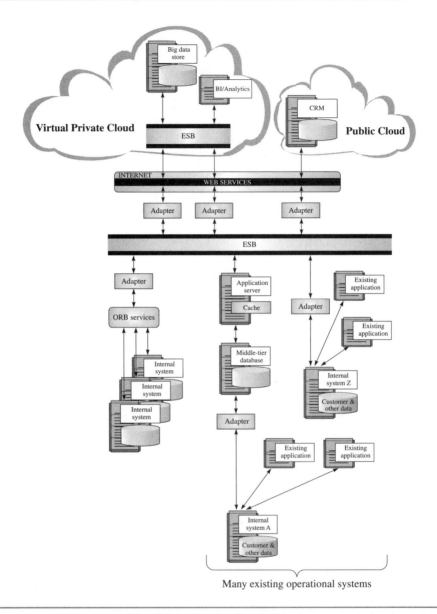

Figure 12.7 Systems used by C.R.'s organization that include a PaaS cloud provider, SaaS cloud provider, and middle-tier persistence.

data services needed changing when the changes to the systems were made. The rest of the services remained unchanged. Presumably, all that was noticed is that the services related to the upgraded systems provided better performance. This is one way

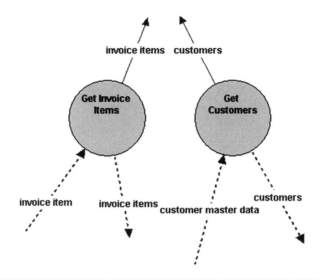

Figure 12.8 Two data services.

C. R.'s organization was able to easily respond to what could be seen as the chaos of business by concentrating work in specific areas, knowing that the structure of the services will keep the system changes isolated.

The structure of the services is what consumers of those services see. They do not see the underlying systems. The design and management of the structure of services is important. Figure 12.9 shows the generated decomposition of services from Figure 10.4. To help think about the structure of the services, they are divided into two layers: business services and data services.[5] The business services layer supports or automates the business functions. The data services layer interacts with the software and hardware systems to access and update data stored in those systems.

Since Figure 12.9 is actually a data flow diagram from the tool used in Chapter 10, it shows only the data flows and not the control flows (requests). Figure 12.10 generalizes Figure 12.9 and adds arrows that represent commands or requests. At the bottom are internal interface services. These could, for example, be the interface for the data services layer mentioned earlier. At the top are external interface services that could be the interface services for the business services layer. These are the interfaces used by many other services, systems, applications, and so on. As will be discussed in the next section on governance, it is important to control or minimize changes to the Web services/messaging that connects these external services.

---

[5] Other variants of the number and names of service layers are used. Nearly all models of service layers include a data service layer.

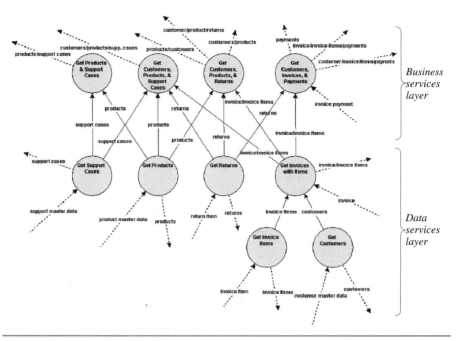

Figure 12.9 Example layers of an SOA.

There could, however, be many services at each layer. So it makes sense to classify services with more detail than layers. Figure 12.11 shows services related to Figure 12.7 organized into collections of services. The circles within the rectangles represent services and each rectangle represents a collection of services.

Notice that no hardware or systems appear in Figure 12.11. Likewise, the services appear the same whether or not they relate to a cloud provider or an internal system.

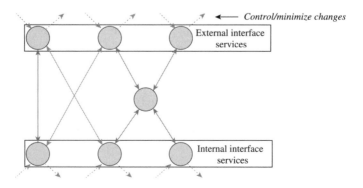

Figure 12.10 Interfaces of services in an SOA.

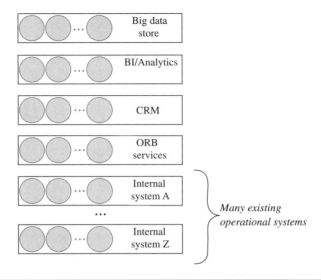

Figure 12.11 Collections of services in an SOA.

If you could enter Figure 12.7 and stand inside the enterprise service bus (ESB), you would see a bunch of services. One way to make sense of those services is to organize them into collections as shown in Figure 12.11.

While you were inside the ESB, you would see that all the services appear to use the same semantic vocabulary and message protocol (SOAP, REST, JSON, etc.). This is why it makes sense to establish a semantic vocabulary as early as possible and to actively maintain it as described in the incremental SOA analysis discussed in Chapter 10 and illustrated in Figure 10.5.

SOA Governance

As you can well imagine, there will be many services in an SOA. Managing those services is an important part of SOA governance. This includes:

- Providing a means to identify services for reuse
- Managing access to services by various entities/services/users
- Monitoring usage of services by various entities/services/users
- Analyzing the impact of proposed changes to services
- Adhering to messaging standards including appropriate industry-wide standards
- Adhering to semantic vocabularies including appropriate industry-wide semantic vocabularies

- Monitoring the performance and availability of services and the underlying systems and hardware supporting services
- Tracking where services run in the supporting systems and hardware

I'm going to dwell a bit on the last bullet. Services are code. They can be written in any language. They can run anywhere code can run. Often, this is an application server, but that is not a requirement. Part of the design process is to determine the best way to implement a service and part of governance is keeping track of where the services run in the supporting systems and hardware.

Chapter 3 mentioned using a service repository for governance. Details such as tokens mentioned on page 147 can be used for managing access and monitoring usage of services. There are products on the market to aid governance that have features such as these. You should decide what tools you will use for governance early since they will impact the development of services. You will need to take into account such features as tokens (or whatever the products use).

Your organization may also add other areas for governance, such as government regulations, laws, internal architectural principles, and so on.

Summary

This chapter provided design concepts and considerations along with staffing and change issues to take into account when establishing a service-oriented architecture. Using big data in a private cloud and a middle-tier architecture with an internal system, this chapter illustrated how properly designed service interfaces can make it easier for an organization to respond to the chaos of modern business.

It is possible to have an SOA without cloud computing. But with the way technology is moving, it is increasingly likely that most SOAs will use cloud computing. Chapter 13 provides suggestions for getting started with cloud computing.

Getting Started with Cloud Computing

Contents

Chapter 12 discussed the importance of service-oriented architecture (SOA) governance given the likely expansion of services within an organization. That expansion pales when you consider the growing number external services in the cloud that are available to any given organization. If you are going to include external services in your SOA, you need to establish a way to evaluate those services and the systems and hardware that support those services. A data center provides the systems and hardware. This chapter provides an overview of how to evaluate external services and data centers for cloud computing.

Expand Your Internal SOA to Include External Services

At this point, you will have the choice of weaving together services from other organizations with services your organization uniquely provides. This is where you could, for example, integrate an external customer relationship management (CRM) service, much like what was described in the initial story about C. R.'s business trip.

STAFFING ISSUES

If you have been experimenting with Web services and incrementally adding new services, you may very well be sailing along. You might have several teams involved with weaving together services. The team members' skills position you to be ready to change things quickly should there be a business need for changing some aspect of your SOA in a hurry.

LIKELY CHANGE ISSUES

The most likely change issues you will encounter at this point are:

- **Not invented here**—As time goes on, more and more external services will be available that could replace internal custom-built services. Be prepared to continue to address this resistance through proper communication of the advantages of these services to your organization.
- **Our problems are special**—This change issue is related to the previous one. It is difficult for many people to realize that specific problems are not special. The opportunity lies in weaving together "not-so-special" services into a special architecture for your organization.

Governance Considerations

Part of governance related to cloud computing is deciding which cloud-based services are critical and which are not. In C.R.'s business trip, services that support his travel (e.g., airlines, trains, and so on) are critical. It is important to really care about availability of those services. On the other hand, services that help C.R. with life experiences (e.g., art, museums, menu translation, and so on) are less critical. If one of those services happens to be unavailable it might be very frustrating, but it is not critical to his business trip.

Of course, for some of the critical services you just need to assume they have high availability. For example, your organization does not have much choice but to assume that cloud-based services provided by an airline or car rental agency will be highly available.

For those critical services where you have a choice of cloud providers, there are issues in addition to those discussed with SOA governance that started on page 161. There are legal, business, and technical issues.

LEGAL ISSUES

You will need to work with a legal team on what should be in a contract with a cloud provider. Your organization needs to retain the right to its data. You need to consider legal jurisdiction and privacy laws in the location of the data center(s) and details on what will occur at the beginning and end of the contract period. You also need to consider including service standards, notification of changes in the data center, liability for data breaches (e.g., hacking or employee theft of data), disaster recovery, and remedies for when things go wrong.

Finally, you need to know if you have a legal requirement for your data to physically stay within a certain jurisdiction. This will affect your choice of a cloud provider.

BUSINESS ISSUES

A business relationship with a cloud provider is just like any other business relationship. You should have a thorough understanding of the provider's reputation, financial stability, longevity, and management practices related to the running of the data center.

TECHNICAL ISSUES

It is important to understand the tools or dashboards available related to the cloud-based service. Establish an agreement on change management for the services provided. You need to understand the technical aspects of how the cloud provider supports high availability. This includes how they provide for redundancy and failover should the data center experience an incident such as a massive power failure in the geographic area in which it is located. You need a thorough understanding of the cloud provider's security and how you can best protect your data in their system.

Data Center Considerations

It is important to realize the significant role the data center plays in cloud computing. Figure 13.1 illustrates some basic features for the data center. It is often a large facility with rows upon rows of rack-mounted hardware running software that allows for the provisioning of virtual machines/servers that make all the resources such as storage appear as if locally attached.

The dynamic nature of provisioning gives rise to the terms *scalability* and *elasticity* for the number of virtual machines/servers and the amount of allocated storage. Of course, as shown in this figure, all this backs up what logically looks like a collection of services, as illustrated by the circles representing a collection of CRM services.

Depending on how you plan to use the services from a cloud provider, you need to take into consideration issues related to availability, disaster recovery, business stability, and legal arrangements.

Availability Issues

Failover is automatically switching to a backup or standby. This could be hardware (virtual or physical) such as a server, network, or disk. It could be failover for software such as an application server, messaging such as a router or enterprise service bus (ESB), a database management system, or custom software for the service. Failover could involve the entire data center so that a backup data center is available.

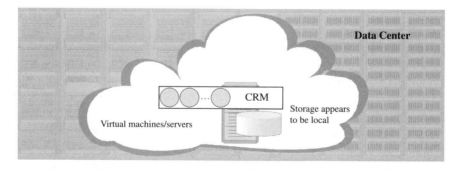

Figure 13.1 Data center with virtual machines/servers behind a collection of services.

You should work with your technical team to create availability requirements necessary for your organization. (I will provide more on availability later in this chapter.)

DISASTER RECOVERY ISSUES

Analyze the disaster recovery plan for the data center. Some possibilities to consider here are the geographic location, type of physical construction, physical security, power sources, power backup, and virtual/software-based security. Again, work with your technical team to develop what your organization might need for disaster recovery. There are publications that go into the technical issues to consider that are related to disaster recovery.

Examples of Technical Issues Related to Availability

Availability can be achieved in multiple ways. There is a lot to consider for availability. This section will give you a few examples of the technical issues to consider. Again, you should work with your technical team members to create availability requirements necessary for your organization

FAILOVER OPTIONS FOR MESSAGING AND DATABASES

As mentioned earlier, the process of a secondary machine taking over for a primary machine is known as *failover*. Listed here are three types of failover that apply to messaging (message routers or ESBs) and databases. The terminology for types of failover can vary.

- **Transparent copy**—the second machine takes over without the knowledge of the application.
- **Transparent cluster**—in a clustered environment, if one node goes down, the remaining node(s) take over for the failed node without the knowledge of the application.
- **Application/service**—the application/service needs to detect the loss of the master and switch to the second machine.

The first two forms of failover are acceptable for an SOA, but the third form, *application/service*, is not in most cases. It would require applications/services that depend on a machine being available to detect the loss of the machine. This would mean, for example, that messaging would need to detect that the primary machine for a master database has failed and then route data to the secondary machine. Conversely, the machine handling the master database would need to detect the loss of the primary machine used for messaging and route data to the secondary machine. This detection of machine loss among disparate components of an SOA is too intertwined.

DATABASE AVAILABILITY OPTIONS

Much like messaging, there are basic options for databases that need to be considered. These are shown in Figure 13.2.

A basic database management system is shown in the lower-left quadrant. As with any database management system, it will protect all data that is successfully updated even if the machine on which it is running should fail. Nevertheless, this does not provide for a secondary machine to take over should the primary machine fail. It also does not provide options for *load leveling* through using more than one machine. Load leveling spreads activity or *load* across more than one machine.

The lower-right quadrant shows a database management system that uses replication. It provides for a secondary machine to take over should the primary machine fail. The data is replicated, which means, depending on the type of replication, data will be available on the secondary machine should it need to take over when the primary machine fails. (Replication options will be covered in the next section.)

The two upper quadrants each show a distributed database, which is one way to load level access to the database. Databases can be distributed in the same location or

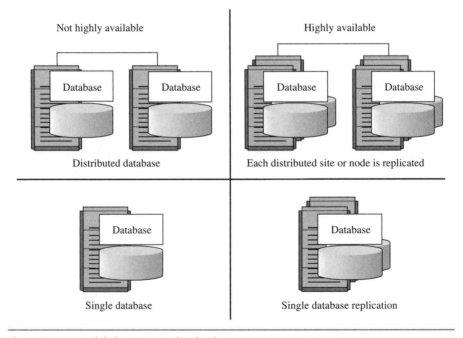

Figure 13.2 Availability options for database management systems.

in separate geographical locations. It is really a design issue. Not every system needs a distributed database, which can add complexity to a system. Nevertheless, there are architectures that can benefit from distributed databases.

The upper-right quadrant shows a distributed database management system that also uses database replication at each node in the distributed database. This is one way to achieve both load leveling of database access and high availability through database replication.

Much like messaging, if the availability of the data in a master database is critical to your organization, then you should consider database replication to make the database highly available. (By the way, Figure 13.2 shows one replicated database in the right quadrant. Many products allow more than one replicated database if that should be needed for your architecture.)

Similarly, if the master database management system is not performing sufficiently on access speed, then distributing the data among multiple machines is an option for load leveling this access.

REPLICATION OPTIONS FOR MESSAGING AND DATABASES

Both messaging (message routers or ESBs) and databases could take advantage of replicated data. Four types of data replication are listed here. The terminology for types of replication can vary. For this reason, each term is also defined in the right of Figure 13.2.

- **Real time**—replication occurs as part of a transaction.
- **Store and forward**—replication occurs on a periodic basis.
- **Time based**—replication occurs at a set time of day.
- **Event based**—replication occurs at a specific event.

The only type of replication that will guarantee that no data is lost at time of failover is real-time replication. All the other forms can lose some data at failover time in one way or another. Real-time replication, however, has a cost. It may double the time it takes to update the stored data in either a messaging system or a database. Nevertheless, if it is important to your architecture that no data be "lost" due to failover, then real-time replication is the only way to go.

Other options concerning replication have to do with how the primary and secondary sites can be used. Some systems allow only updates on the primary site (sometimes called *master site*). The secondary (or *slave* or *replicated*) site exists only to receive the secondary update. Other systems allow data to be updated on either the primary or secondary site. The first master-slave technique is simpler. The second technique may open up architectural opportunities. A lot depends on your organization's needs to determine which would be more useful.

Cloud Brokers

Sometimes it can be helpful to employ a cloud broker to help you sort through your options for cloud computing. Cloud brokers act more or less like mortgage brokers. They evaluate your cloud computing needs and provide you with a choice of cloud providers that best meet those needs. A cautionary note here is to ensure that you are working with an independent cloud broker. When a cloud broker is affiliated with a cloud provider, it raises doubt that you are getting choices that best meet your needs.

Should You Be Your Own Cloud Provider?

Your organization can be its own cloud provider, but you need to weigh the technical and business issues to take this on. As opposed to an external cloud provider where you pay for resources as you use them, you will need to invest upfront in the hardware and software for the data center. Of course, there can be legal or business reasons that you would want to do this.

There are options that can make this technically easier, such as "cloud computing in a box," which creates a fully configured data center for your organization. Sometimes, it is possible to find a leasing option for such a "box" so that you can minimize your upfront costs.

You need to consider issues of availability. For example, will you need software that provides for replication and failover within you data center? Will you need to maintain a second, replicated data center should your primary data center fail for some reason?

In any case, you will need to invest in the people who maintain your data center and keep it secure. What you can offer people in the way of technical challenge and compensation will affect how well you can staff your data center. This is one area where an external cloud provider might have an easier time maintaining the staff necessary to properly maintain a cloud data center.

Summary

This chapter discussed the expanded role of governance related to cloud computing. As part of that governance, it is important establish a way to evaluate cloud-based services and the data centers that support those services. This chapter highlighted issues of availability related to cloud computing. At the end, it presented issues to consider if your organization wants to become a cloud provider.

Chapter 14

Revisiting the Business Trip in the Not-Too-Distant Future

Contents

Let's revisit C. R.'s business trip described in Chapters 1 and 2 to summarize the Web services, service-oriented architectures (SOAs), and cloud computing related to the business trip. Page references appear within parentheses indicating where you can find more information on the topic in this book.

Services for C. R.'s Business Trip

Chapter 2 provided an introduction to the technology used for C. R.'s business trip. Figure 14.1 is a redrawing of Figure 2.1 from Chapter 2 to show the services and interconnections used to plan and manage his trip.

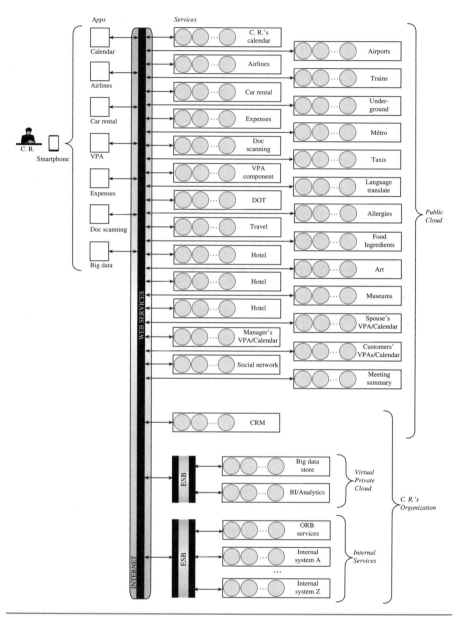

Figure 14.1 Details of services and data interchange related to C. R.'s business trip.

In all likelihood, there are probably many hundreds of services used in C. R.'s business trip. There are also multiple SOAs assembled from the services. Figure 14.1 shows the collections of services (see page 160). The services are represented in the figure as circles. The collections are represented by the rectangles around the circles.

Notice how everything is connected using Web services (see page 19) within the Internet. In Figure 14.1, the Internet is represented by the vertical shaded area. Web services are shown as a black line within the shaded area. This represents that Web services messaging protocols (SOAP, REST, JSON, etc.) are a subset of all protocols that can be used on the Internet.

There are two enterprise service buses (ESBs) in the figure (see page 62). One is a specialized ESB for the services available related to the big data store and the business information (BI)/analytics in a virtual private cloud. In addition to facilitating the message passing within the virtual private cloud, the ESB also acts as a gateway to the Internet for the services in this particular virtual private cloud (see page 42).

The second ESB in the figure is used by the internal services for C. R.'s organization. Similar to the ESB in the virtual private cloud, this ESB is used for facilitating the message passing among the internal services in C. R.'s organization. It also acts as a gateway to the Internet. C. R's organization defined a standard semantic vocabulary (see page 29) to use with its ESB. This means that from within this ESB, all services appear to use the same vocabulary and communication protocol, including external services that are in the public cloud, through the use of adapters (see page 63).

Other collections of services in Figure 14.1 may use an ESB. You can use those services without knowing whether or not the service uses an ESB. All you need to know is the top-level service interface they present to the Internet via Web services.

The smartphone applications at the left in the figure represent only the applications that were mentioned in the business trip story. C. R. undoubtedly has more applications than this on his smartphone.

What you don't see in Figure 14.1 is any hardware. Presumably, everything in the figure executes on virtual machines/servers in data centers (see page 166). The services could be moved to different data centers and there would be no change in the figure. Where the services actually execute is technically not important. There can be legal and other nontechnical reasons for caring where data centers are located.

The data centers are what underlie cloud computing from cloud providers. One of the features that distinguishes cloud computing from just a data center is that cloud computing provides *elasticity*: "Capabilities can be elastically provisioned and released, in some cases automatically, to scale rapidly outward and inward commensurate with demand. To the consumer, the capabilities available for provisioning often appear to be unlimited and can be appropriated in any quantity at any time."[1]

Nearly all the services in the figure are software as a service (SaaS) cloud providers (see page 42). For example, the customer relationship management (CRM)

---

[1] Peter Mell and Timothy Grance, *The NIST Definition of Cloud Computing: Recommendations of the National Institute of Standards and Technology*, NIST Special Publication 800-145, Sept. 2011, p. 2.

service and the document scanning service used by C.R. on his business trip are SaaS. These are the cloud provider's own or custom software.

The big data store and the BI/analytics software were implemented using a platform as a service (PaaS) virtual private cloud provider (see page 42). That software was developed by C.R.'s organization using a cloud provider's development tools and a NoSQL database management system. C.R.'s organization realized that it needed the capabilities of a cloud (elasticity of resources, high availability, etc.) for storing and analyzing this data but did not want to build a data center to provide all the features of a cloud-computing environment. This way, it only pays for resources that it uses rather than investing upfront in the capabilities and a cloud and the ongoing management costs.

C.R.'s organization retrofitted many of its internal systems to act as services and use the internal ESB. Note that the internal systems are not in any type of cloud. They are probably supported using a data center run by C.R.'s organization. But C.R.'s organization did not see a reason to create a private cloud for its internal services.

The collections of services shown in this figure were used to build multiple SOAs. C.R.'s organization has an SOA that includes the collections of the services at the bottom in the figure. Its SOA mixes public and virtual private cloud computing with the non-cloud computing of its internal data center. Many of the services shown may also have their own SOAs. Among those that might include the airlines, car rental agencies, and the local department of transportation (DOT). The VPA component also undoubtedly has a sophisticated SOA.

Figure 14.1 allows for more connections than were shown in Figure 2.1 because everything is connected using Web services. So, given the correct authorizations/permissions, other capabilities could be constructed. For example, there could be a new service created out of services from the airlines, car rental agencies, hotels, museums, and art that would be a specialized travel service that creates custom travel arrangements for people interested in specific types of art.

▊ The Future for C. R.'s Organization

What is likely to happen at C.R.'s organization as the remaining existing systems age? Will the organization take advantage of the services interface it has in place for these systems and upgrade the hardware and software that is "under" that interface? The other option his organization would have is to maintain that interface but move more of the processing to the cloud. Will it move most of the processing to the cloud and pay for resources as it uses them? A lot probably depends on the experience the organization has with cloud computing and the ongoing development of standards that could make the use of cloud computing more enticing.

Summary

This chapter tied much of the technology of Web services, service-oriented architectures, and cloud computing back to the story of C.R.'s business trip in Chapters 1 and 2. It provided an overview and summary for much of the material that is in this book.

Reference Guide

Part V provides a reference guide for the book. Chapter 15 lists the various semantic vocabularies. Chapter 16 is a guide to terminology related to Web services, service-oriented architectures, and cloud computing.

Chapter 15

Semantic Vocabularies

Contents

Every industry group has its own vocabulary for its activities. Various industry groups have been developing formal semantic vocabularies to take advantage of the Web services messaging protocols. Originally, many of these vocabularies were referred to as *XML vocabularies*.

Common Semantic Vocabularies

This is a listing of semantic vocabularies that can be shared among multiple industries or disciplines. New vocabularies are continually being developed and some vocabularies go away.

ADDRESS XML

Address Data Interchange Specification (ADIS): XML specification for the interchange of address data both domestically and internationally. It is based on storing the parts of an address, or address elements, and then combining them together with intelligent editing to create output formats, or renditions, for particular mail pieces. It includes data about the addresses, such as whether they are complete or missing particular elements that affect address quality.

eXtensible Name Address Language (xNAL): XML specification for managing name and address data regardless of country of origin. It consists of two parts: xNL, eXtensible Name Language, to define the name components, and xAL, eXtensible Address Language, to define the address components. xNL and xAL are part of the OASIS Customer Information Quality (CIQ) family of specifications.

Mail.XML: XML specification for communication between industry members and from industry to the final mail processing and delivery organization that delivers the mail to the end consumer (e.g., USPS).

COMPUTING ENVIRONMENT XML

Application Vulnerability Description Language (AVDL): An XML definition for exchange of information relating to security vulnerabilities of applications exposed to networks.

Intrusion Detection Message Exchange Format (IDMEF): Data formats and exchange procedures for sharing information of interest to intrusion detection and response systems and to management systems that may need to interact with them.

Web-Based Enterprise Management (WBEM) Initiative: A set of management and Internet standard technologies developed to unify the management of enterprise computing environments. WBEM provides the ability for the industry to deliver a well-integrated set of standard-based management tools leveraging the emerging Web technologies. The DMTF has developed a core set of standards that make up WBEM, which includes a data model, the common information model (CIM) standard; an encoding specification, xmlCIM Encoding Specification; and a transport mechanism, CIM operations over HTTP. The CIM specification is the language and methodology for describing management data. The CIM schema includes models for systems, applications, networks (LAN), and devices. The CIM schema will enable applications from different developers on different platforms to describe management data in a standard format so that it can be shared among a variety of management applications.

The xmlCIM Encoding Specification defines XML elements, written in document type definition (DTD), which can be used to represent CIM classes and instances. The CIM operations over HTTP specifications define a mapping of CIM operations onto HTTP that allows implementations of CIM to interoperate in an open, standardized manner and completes the technologies that support WBEM.

Web Services Distributed Management (WSDM): This specifies the Web services architecture and technology to manage distributed resources. It includes a model of a Web service as a manageable resource.

Web Application Security (WAS): This specification includes:

- A classification scheme for Web security vulnerabilities.
- A model to provide guidance for initial threat, impact, and therefore risk ratings.
- An XML schema to describe Web security conditions that can be used by both assessment and protection tools.

CONTENT SYNDICATION XML

Information and Content Exchange (ICE): XML specification that, for content providers, standardizes the process for setting up subscribers and for delivering and managing subscriber content. For content subscribers, ICE standardizes the process for setting up a subscription and for automated content retrieval. The ICE specification provides businesses with an XML-based common language and architecture that facilitates automatic exchanging, updating, supplying, and controlling of assets in a trusted fashion without manual packaging or knowledge of remote website structures.

Real Simple Syndication (RSS): RSS is a dialect of XML for content syndication. Some say the acronym also stands for "Rich Site Summary."

CUSTOMER INFORMATION XML

eXtensible Customer Information Language (xCIL): Uses customer data such as telephone numbers, email addresses, account numbers, credit card numbers, etc. to uniquely identify a customer. This helps in achieving a single customer view, customer relationship management (CRM) strategies, understanding a customer profile, etc. xCIL is part of the OASIS Customer Information Quality (CIQ) family of specifications.

eXtensible Customer Relationships Language (xCRL): XML standard specification to represent customer relationships in a standard way to help achieve interoperability between different systems, processes, and platforms, and in building effective single-customer views. xNAL and xCIL are referenced by xCRL.

Electronic Data Interchange (EDI) XML

XML/EDI: XML specification to exchange different types of data (e.g., an invoice, healthcare claim, or project status). It includes implementing EDI dictionaries and online repositories to business language, rules, and objects.

Geospatial XML

City Geography Markup Language (CityGML): XML specification for the representation, storage, and exchange of virtual three-dimensional (3D) city and landscape models. CityGML is implemented as an application schema of the Geography Markup Language (see next). CityGML models both complex and geo-referenced 3D vector data along with the semantics associated with the data. CityGML is based on a general-purpose information model in addition to geometry and appearance information. For specific domain areas, CityGML also provides an extension mechanism to enrich the data with identifiable features while preserving semantic interoperability.

Geography Markup Language (GML): XML specification for expressing geographical features. GML serves as a modeling language for geographic systems as well as an open interchange format for geographic transactions on the Internet. A GML document allows users and developers to describe generic geographic data sets that contain points, lines, and polygons. The developers of GML envision communities working to define community-specific application schemas that are specialized extensions of GML. Using application schemas, users can refer to roads, highways, and bridges instead of points, lines, and polygons. If everyone in a community agrees to use the same schemas, they can exchange data more easily.

OGC Web Services (OWS): XML specification to extend and "ruggedize" existing and draft OpenGIS standards into a robust and complete interoperability framework for implementing multivendor enterprise—and enterprise-to-enterprise—solutions in government and business.

OpenGIS Location Services (OpenLS): XML specification to define access to the core services and abstract data types (ADTs) that comprise the GeoMobility Server, an open location services platform. Abstract data types are encoded in XML for location services (XLS). XLS is defined as the method for encoding request/response messages and associated abstract data types for the GeoMobility Server. The interfaces allow telecommunications companies, telematics service providers, traditional GIS technology companies, and location-based services (LBSs) providers to implement interoperable LBS applications that access multiple content repositories and service frameworks that work across many different wireless networks and devices.

Human XML

HumanML: XML schema and Resource Description Framework (RDF) schema specification containing sets of modules that frame and embed contextual human characteristics, including physical, cultural, social, kinesic, psychological, and intentional features within conveyed information.

Localization XML

XML Localization Interchange File Format (XLIFF): XLIFF is an extensible specification for the interchange of localization information. The specification provides the ability to mark up and capture localizable data and interoperate with different processes or phases without loss of information. The vocabularies are tool neutral and support the localization-related aspects of internationalization and the entire localization process. The vocabularies support common software and content data formats.

Math XML

MathML: XML specification for describing mathematical notation and capturing both its structure and content. The goal of MathML is to enable mathematics to be served, received, and processed on the Internet, just as HTML has enabled this functionality for text.

OpenMath: XML specification for representing mathematical objects with their semantics, allowing them to be exchanged between computer programs, stored in databases, or published on the World Wide Web. There is a strong relationship to the MathML recommendation from the World Wide Web Consortium (W3C) and a large overlap between the two developer communities. MathML deals principally with the presentation of mathematical objects, while OpenMath is solely concerned with their semantic meaning or content. While MathML does have some limited facilities for dealing with content, it also allows semantic information encoded in OpenMath to be embedded inside a MathML structure. Thus, the two specifications may be seen as complementary.

Open Mathematical Documents (OMDoc): XML specification for representing the semantics and structure of various kinds of mathematical documents, including articles, textbooks, interactive books, and courses. OMDoc is an extension of the OpenMath and MathML standards, and in particular of the content part of MathML.

eXtensible Data Format (XDF): XML specification of common scientific data format and general mathematical principles that can be used throughout the scientific disciplines. It includes these key features: hierarchical data structures, any dimensional arrays merged with coordinate information, high-dimensional tables merged with field information, variable resolution, easy wrapping of existing data, user-specified coordinate systems, searchable ASCII metadata, and extensibility to new features/data formats.

OPEN APPLICATIONS GROUP INTEGRATION SPECIFICATION (OAGIS)

Open Applications Group Integration Specification (OAGIS): OAGIS defines a common content model and common messages for communication between business applications. This includes application-to-application (A2A) and business-to-business (B2B) integration.

OPEN OFFICE XML

Open Office XML: The OpenDocument Format (ODF) is an open XML-based document file format for office applications to be used for documents containing text, spreadsheets, charts, and graphical elements. It is intended to meet the following requirements:

- It must be suitable for office documents containing text, spreadsheets, charts, and graphical documents.
- It must be compatible with the W3C eXtensible Markup Language (XML) v1.0 and W3C Namespaces in XML v1.0 specifications.
- It must retain high-level information suitable for editing the document.
- It must be friendly to transformations using XSLT or similar XML-based languages or tools.
- It should keep the document's content and layout information separate such that they can be processed independently of each other.
- It should "borrow" from similar, existing standards wherever possible and permitted.

TOPIC MAPS XML

Topic Maps Published Subjects for Geography and Languages (GeoLang): GeoLang advances the use of the XML Topic Maps specification (ISO/IEC 13250:2000) for navigating information resources by defining published subjects for languages, countries, and regions. Languages, countries, and regions are subjects that occur frequently across a wide range of topic maps. To promote maximum reusability, interchangeability, and mergability, standardized sets of published subjects are required to cover these domains.

TRADE XML

Controlled Trade Markup Language (CTML): XML specification of unified trade control vocabulary that supports an international collection of business documents (e.g, trade applications, cases, licenses, delivery verification certificates, etc.) through the extension and expansion of an existing XML vocabulary.

Translation XML

Translation Web Services: The intent is that any publisher of content to be translated should be able to automatically connect to and use the services of any translation vendor over the Internet without any previous direct communication between the two.

Universal Business Language (UBL)

Universal Business Language (UBL): This is an important development in the use of XML vocabularies. In any human language, the same word can mean different things for different industries. Conversely, different words sometimes can mean the same thing in different industries. The OASIS UBL Technical Committee's charter is to define a common XML business document library. UBL will provide a set of XML building blocks and a framework that will enable trading partners to unambiguously identify and exchange business documents in specific contexts. This is an effort to unite efforts underway by organizations and standards groups around the world. The OASIS UBL Technical Committee intends to enhance and harmonize overlapping XML business libraries and similar technologies to advance consensus on an international standard.

Universal Data Element Framework (UDEF)

Universal Data Element Framework (UDEF): This is a cross-industry metadata identification strategy designed to facilitate convergence and interoperability among e-business and other standards. The objective of UDEF is to provide a means of real-time identification for semantic equivalency as an attribute to data elements within e-business document and integration formats. The supporters of UDEF hope that it can be seen as the "Dewey Decimal System" across standards. UDEF can be seen as only an attribute in the data element. There are no process, validation, or handling requirements. The intent is to communicate in a standard and repeatable way the exact concept that the data element represents. There is very little about context— just enough to identify the data element exactly.

Specific Semantic Vocabularies

This is a listing of semantic vocabularies that are specific to a particular industry or discipline. New vocabularies are continually being developed and some vocabularies go away.

ACCOUNTING XML

Small and Medium-Sized Business XML (smbXML): XML specification for describing business transactions. smbXML is specifically designed for the needs of the small-to medium-sized business community.

ADVERTISING XML

AdsML Framework: A set of XML specifications along with workflow and best practices designed to implement e-commerce communications for the buying, selling, delivering, receiving, invoicing, and paying of advertisements. All of the standards in the framework share both an e-commerce philosophy and a common set of design principles; they use common names and structures; and they support a common message choreography. The AdsML Framework aims to support all kinds of advertising, in all media, and through all stages of the lifecycle of an advertisement. Specifications for Publisher & Agency Communications Exchange XML (SPACE/XML): XML specification for electronic business transactions related to:

- Space reservations
- Insertion orders
- Creative materials
- Job tickets
- Invoices

The standard was developed to get paid faster from a reduction in information errors that cause billing discrepancies. Additionally, the goal was to create the specifications for ad insertion orders to eliminate much of the confusion and misinformation that can result when insertion orders are sent by fax or mail. By establishing this set of standards, any publication or agency could receive electronic business information from any collaborative partner.

In 2005, IDEAlliance merged the SPACE specification into the AdsML Framework (see above).

ASTRONOMY XML

Flexible Image Transport System Markup Language (FITSML): XML specification for astronomical data, such as images, spectra, tables, and sky atlases.

BUILDING XML

oBIX: The Open Building Information Exchange specification that will enable enterprise applications to communicate with mechanical and electrical systems in buildings.

CHEMISTRY XML

Chem eStandards: XML specification for data exchange developed specifically for the buying, selling, and delivery of chemicals.

Chemical Markup Language (CML): XML specification covering macromolecular sequences to inorganic molecules and quantum chemistry.

CONSTRUCTION XML

Architecture Description Markup Language (ADML): XML specification for architecture. ADML is based on ACME, an architecture description language. ADML adds to ACME, a standardized representation of the ability to define links to objects outside the architecture (e.g., rationale, designs, and components).

EDUCATION XML

Schools Interoperability Framework (SIF): An XML specification for data sharing among schools, kindergarten through twelfth grade.

FINANCE XML

eXtensible Business Reporting Language (XBRL): XML specification that describes financial information for public and private companies and other organizations. They have created XML taxonomies. Since financial reporting varies by country, the taxonomies vary by country.

Financial Information eXchange (FIX) Protocol: XML specification for the real-time electronic exchange of securities transactions.

Financial Products Markup Language (FpML): XML specification for swaps, derivatives, and structured financial products.

Interactive Financial Exchange (IFX): XML specification for electronic bill presentment and payment, business-to-business payments, business-to-business banking (e.g., balance and transaction reporting, remittance information), automated teller machine communications, consumer-to-business payments, and consumer-to-business banking.

Market Data Definition Language (MDDL): XML specification to enable interchange of data necessary to account for, analyze, and trade instruments of the world's financial markets. MDDL seeks, through definition of common terms, to provide a standard vocabulary so market data may be exchanged unambiguously between exchanges, vendors, redistributors, and subscribers. MDDL is designed to facilitate delivery of all data and to increase ease of processing for recipients of this market-based financial data.

Open Financial Exchange (OFX) XML Schema: XML specification for the electronic exchange of financial data between financial institutions, businesses, and consumers via the Internet. It is designed to support a wide range of financial activities including consumer and small business banking, consumer and small business bill payment, and investments transaction download, including stocks, bonds, and mutual funds.

Research Information eXchange Markup Language (RIXML): XML specification to tag any piece of research content in any form or media with enough detail for end users to be able to quickly search, sort, and filter aggregated research.

Society for Worldwide Interbank Financial Telecommunication (SWIFT): SWIFT Standards develops business standards to support transactions in the financial markets for payments, securities, treasury, and trade services. Their proprietary MT messages are complemented by new XML-based (MX) messages, which enable the transfer of richer data for more complex business transactions.

Food XML

Meat and Poultry XML (mpXML) Schema: XML specification for exchanging business information among all segments and entities in the meat and poultry supply and marketing chain.

Government XML

Election Markup Language (EML): XML specification for the structured interchange of data among hardware, software, and service providers who engage in any aspect of providing election or voter services to public or private organizations. The services performed for such elections include but are not limited to voter role/membership maintenance (new voter registration, membership and dues collection, change of address tracking, etc.), citizen/membership credentialing, redistricting, requests for absentee/expatriate ballots, election calendaring, logistics management (polling place management), election notification, ballot delivery and tabulation, election results reporting, and demographics.

National Information Exchange Model (NIEM): This has been developed through a partnership of the U.S. Department of Justice and the Department of

Homeland Security. It is designed to develop, disseminate, and support enterprise-wide information exchange standards and processes that enable jurisdictions to effectively share critical information in emergency situations, as well as support the day-to-day operations of agencies throughout the United States. NIEM builds on the Global Justice XML Data Model (GJXDM).

Tax XML: This includes a vocabulary of terms and a repository of artifacts including XML templates, documents exchanged for tax compliance, best practices, guidelines, and recommendations for practical implementation. The intent is a common vocabulary that will allow participants to unambiguously identify the tax-related information exchanged within a particular business context.

HEALTHCARE XML

Clinical Data Interchange Standards Consortium (CDISC) Operational Data Model (ODM): XML specification that is a vendor-neutral, platform-independent format for interchange and archive of data collected in clinical trials. The model represents study metadata, data, and administrative data associated with a clinical trial. Only the information that needs to be shared among different software systems during a trial or archived after a trial is included in the model.

Health Level 7 (HL7) Healthcare XML Format: XML specification for the exchange of clinical data and information. The purpose of the exchange of clinical data includes, but is not limited to, provision of clinical care, support of clinical and administrative research, execution of automated transaction-oriented decision logic (medical logic modules), support of outcomes research, support of clinical trials, and support of data reporting to government and other authorized third parties.

HUMAN RESOURCES (HR) XML

HR-XML: XML specification designed to enable e-business and the automation of human-resources related data exchanges.

INSTRUMENTS XML

Instrument Markup Language (IML): XML specification that applies to virtually any kind of instrument that can be controlled by a computer. The approach to instrument description and control apply to many domains, from medical instruments (e.g., microscopes) to printing presses to machine assembly lines. The concepts behind IML apply equally well to the description and control of instruments in general.

Insurance XML

ACORD XML for Life Insurance: XML specification based on the ACORD Life Data Model.

ACORD XML for Property and Casualty Insurance: XML specification that addresses real-time requirement by defining property and casualty transactions that include both request and response messages for personal lines, commercial lines, specialty lines, surety, claims, and accounting transactions.

ACORD XML for Reinsurance and Large Commercial: XML specification that addresses real-time requirements by defining business transactions that include both request and response messages for Personal Lines, Commercial Lines, Specialty Lines, Surety, Claims, and Accounting transactions.

Legal XML

Global Justice XML Data Model (Global JXDM): XML standards that enable the justice and public safety community to effectively share information at all levels—laying the foundation for local, state, and national justice interoperability.

LegalXML eContracts: Open XML standards for the markup of contract documents to enable the efficient creation, maintenance, management, exchange, and publication of contract documents and contract terms.

LegalXML Electronic Court Filing: XML standards to create legal documents and transmit legal documents from an attorney, party, or self-represented litigant to a court, from a court to an attorney, from a party or self-represented litigant to another court, and from an attorney or other user to another attorney or other user of legal documents.

LegalXML eNotary: An agreed set of technical requirements to govern self-proving electronic legal information.

LegalXML Integrated Justice: XML standards for exchanging data among justice system branches and agencies.

LegalXML Legal Transcripts: XML standards for the syntax to represent legal transcript documents either as stand-alone structured content or as part of other legal records.

LegalXML Legislative Documents: XML standards for the markup of legislative documents and a system of simple citation capability for nonlegislative documents (e.g., newspaper articles). The primary goal is to allow the public to more easily participate in the democratic process by creating a more open, accessible, easier to parse, research, and reference legislative documents.

LegalXML Online Dispute Resolution (OdrXML): XML standard for the markup of information and documents used in online dispute resolution systems. The primary goal is to allow the public to gain standardized access to justice through private and government-sponsored dispute resolution systems.

LegalXML Subscriber Data Handover Interface (SDHI): XML standards for the production of consistent Subscriber Data Handover Interface (SDHI) by telecommunications or Internet service providers, concerning a subscriber or communications identifier (e.g., a telephone number) in response to an XML-structured request that includes, when necessary, authorization from a judicial, public safety, or law enforcement authority.

MANUFACTURING XML

papiNet: The papiNet standard is a set of XML message standards for the paper and forest industry. papiNet provides a common messaging interface so that companies will no longer need to negotiate and agree on data definitions and formats with each trading partner, a costly and arduous task. The papiNet standards are compatible with other important open standards like ebXML.

Planning and Scheduling Language on XML Specification (PSLX): The PSLX specification is a set of XML message standards for information about planning and scheduling in manufacturing industries.

Production Planning and Scheduling (PPS): The specification of common object models and corresponding XML schemas for production planning and scheduling software, which can communicate with each other to establish collaborative planning and scheduling on intra and/or inter-enterprises in manufacturing industries.

NEWS XML

News Industry Text Format (NITF): XML specification for the content and structure of news articles. NITF differs from NewsML in that there is no concept in NewsML of a paragraph or subheadline. Also, there is no concept in NITF of a sidebar or alternative translations of the same document. For text stories, the International Press Telecommunications Council recommends the NITF.

NewsML: XML specification for encoding for news that is intended to be used for the creation, transfer, and delivery of news. NewsML is media independent and allows equally for the representation of the evening TV news and a simple textual story.

Publishing Requirements for Industry Standard Markup (PRISM): XML metadata vocabulary for managing, postprocessing, multipurposing, and aggregating publishing content for magazine and journal publishing.

SportsML: XML specification for the interchange of sports data.

OIL AND GAS XML

Petroleium Industry Data Exchange (PIDX) standards: PIDX has developed and published several XML specifications that support automation of various aspects of the oil and gas supply chain. PIDX also developed a library of EDI X12 and FTP standards that are used to support oil and gas business.

PHOTO XML

Common Picture eXchange environment (CPXe): XML specification that enables the transmission of digital pictures and order and commerce information between digital cameras, PCs, desktop software, Internet services, photo kiosks, digital minilabs, and photofinishers, regardless of the type of digital camera, device, PC brand, operating system, or photofinishing equipment used by service providers. By incorporating CPXe, photographic device and software vendors give their customers easy connection to a range of digital photography services.

PHYSICS XML

Common Data Format Markup Language (CDFML): XML specification that is a self-describing data abstraction for the storage and manipulation of multidimensional data in a discipline-independent fashion.

PUBLISHING XML

DocBook: XML/SGML vocabulary particularly well suited to books and papers about computer hardware and software (though it is by no means limited to these applications).

PROSE/XML: XML specification intended to be a standardized method for publishers to communicate job specifications to commercial printers. In as far as it enforces certain formats for its data, and thereby standardizes the "look" of the data, the PROSE/XML specification rarely defines its content data values. It is left up to the trading partners to determine the proper values for the content data transmitted via the PROSE/XML specification.

Shipment and Logistics Specification (SnL): XML message specification for efficient communication among those providing delivery instructions, transportation planning, and distribution services for shipment of printed product. SnL is made up of a family of related specifications. These specifications include shipment plans, shipment notifications, print order messages, and goods receipt messages.

XML Book Industry Transaction Standards (XBITS): This is a working group of IDEAlliance and a Book Industry Study Group (BISG)/ Book Industry Standards and Communications (BISAC) publisher and manufacturer committee that is designing standard XML transactions to facilitate bidirectional electronic data exchanges between publishers, printers, paper mills, and component vendors.

REAL ESTATE XML

Mortgage Industry Standards Maintenance Organization (MISMO): XML specification for commercial mortgage origination data that provides both the content and format for borrowers and mortgage bankers to transmit data to lenders.

Real Estate Transaction Standard (RETS): XML specification for exchanging real estate transaction information.

TELECOMMUNICATIONS XML

Parlay X Web Services: The Parlay application programming interfaces (APIs) are designed to enable creation of telephony applications as well as to "telecom-enable" IT applications. The Parlay X Web services are intended to stimulate the development of next-generation network applications by IT developers who are not necessarily experts in telephony or telecommunications.

Telecommunications Interchange Markup (TIM): XML specification for describing the structure of telecommunications and other technical documents.

TRAVEL XML

The OpenTravel Alliance (OTA): XML specification that serves as a common language for travel-related terminology and a mechanism for promoting the exchange of information across all travel industry segments.

Terminology

Contents

This chapter serves as a quick reference to terminology related to Web services, service-oriented architecture (SOA), or cloud computing. For those entries that have related examples or more information in this book, there is a page reference to where you can find the additional information.

Since this is a dynamic area, new and revised technologies and concepts will be occurring regularly. If you cannot find what you need here, go to *http://www.service-architecture.com/*.

Adapters

Adapters allow Web services connections with internally developed systems or packaged software, usually with an enterprise service bus (ESB). There can also be adapters between Web services and CORBA or DCOM. See page 63.

Agents

Agents are active entities that work with Web services. On a relatively simple side, there are agents that can help us shop online. More sophisticated agents would be able to perform negotiations, monitor the status of systems, or monitor changes in the content of databases or other systems. These agents could communicate with each other or with other systems internal or external to the organization using Web services. The virtual personal assistant mentioned throughout this book is an agent.

Analytics

Analytics is the discovery of patterns in data. See also Business Intelligence (BI).

Application Programming Interface (API)

API provides a means for software components to communicate with each other. In the context of SOAs, these APIs use Web services, such as SOAP, REST, and JSON. See page 39.

Application Server

An application server is a component-based product that resides in the middle tier of an architecture. It provides middleware services for security and state maintenance, along with data access and persistence. See page 153.

Atomic Service

An atomic service is a well-defined, self-contained function that does not depend on the context or state of other services. See page 31.

Big Data

Big data is data that requires some capacity that is beyond that of a traditional database system. There may be too much data (sometimes referred to as *volume of data*). The data is created at a very high speed (sometimes referred to as *velocity of data*). The data may be unstructured and there may be various types of structured and unstructured data—audio, video, sensor feeds, unstructured text, and so on (sometimes referred to as *variety of data*).

Business Intelligence (BI)

BI software is a broad area covering data mining, pattern finding, reporting, and event detection among other possible functions. Often, BI is used with data warehouses and big data stores, but that is not a mandatory requirement.

Business Process Execution Language (BPEL)

BPEL defines a notation for specifying business process behavior based on Web services. Business processes can be described in two ways:

- Executable business processes model actual behavior of a participant in a business interaction.
- Business protocols, in contrast, use process descriptions that specify the mutually visible message exchange behavior of each of the parties involved in the protocol without revealing their internal behavior. The process descriptions for business protocols are called *abstract processes*.

BPEL is used to model the behavior of both executable and abstract processes. The scope includes:

- Sequencing of process activities, especially Web service interactions
- Correlation of messages and process instances
- Recovery behavior in case of failures and exceptional conditions
- Bilateral Web service-based relationships between process roles
- Business Process Execution Language for Web Services (BPEL4WS)

Business Process Modeling Notation (BPMN)

The BPMN specification provides a graphical notation for expressing business processes in a business process diagram (BPD). The BPMN specification also provides a binding between the notation's graphical elements and the constructs of block-structured process execution languages, including BPML and BPEL.

Business Process Query Language (BPQL)

BPQL is a management interface to a business process management infrastructure that includes a process execution facility (process server) and a process deployment facility (process repository).

Business Process Specification Schema (BPSS)

BPSS is a standard framework by which business systems may be configured to support execution of business collaborations consisting of business transactions. It is based on prior UN/CEFACT work, specifically the meta model behind the UN/CEFACT Modeling Methodology (UMM) defined in the N090R9.1 specification. The specification schema supports the specification of business transactions and the choreography of business transactions into business collaborations. These patterns determine the actual exchange of business documents and business signals between the partners to achieve the required electronic commerce transaction.

Caching

Caching is the retention of data to minimize network traffic flow and/or disk access. See page 153.

Cloud

Cloud and *cloud computing* are terms likely inspired by the use of clouds in diagrams to represent the Internet. Originally, cloud was a marketing term, but it has gained wide use because it provides a sense of how services, etc. are "out there," somewhere on the Internet or more locally on an organization's intranet. See page 35.

Collaboration Protocol Profile/Agreement (CPP/A)

CPP/A provides interoperability between two parties even though they may use application software and runtime support software from different vendors. CPP defines message-exchange capabilities and the business collaborations that it supports. CPA defines the way two parties will interact in performing the chosen business collaboration.

Community Cloud

A community cloud is more restricted than a public cloud. The restriction is to a "community." The restriction could be based on an industry segment, by general interest, or by whatever way a group might be defined. These clouds could be multitenanted. The underlying data center might be provided by a third party or by one member of the community. See page 41.

Composite Service

A composite service is created by combining services. Composite services are built using an SOA. See page 31.

CORBA

CORBA is the acronym for Common Object Request Broker Architecture. It was developed under the auspices of the Object Management Group (OMG). It is middleware. A CORBA-based program from any vendor on almost any computer, operating system, programming language, and network, can interoperate with a CORBA-based program from the same or another vendor on almost any other computer, operating system, programming language, and network.

The first SOA for many people in the past was with the use of object request brokers (ORBs) based on the CORBA specification. The CORBA specification is responsible for really increasing the awareness of SOAs. See page 57.

Data Cleansing

Data cleansing is changes made to improve data quality. For existing data being loaded into a data mart or data warehouse, extract, transform, and load (ETL) software could be used to improve the quality of the data. See page 61.

Data Warehouse

A data warehouse often refers to combining data from many different sources across an enterprise. It is also referred to as enterprise data warehouse (EDW). The development of data warehouses usually involves ETL software. See page 138.

DCOM

DCOM is the acronym for Distributed Component Object Model, an extension of Component Object Model (COM). DCOM was introduced in 1996 and is designed for use across multiple network transports, including Internet protocols such as HTTP. DCOM is based on the Open Software Foundation's DCE-RPC spec and will work with both Java applets and ActiveX components through its use of the COM. It works primarily with Microsoft Windows. See page 57.

ebXML Registry

The ebXML registry is similar to UDDI in that it allows businesses to find one another, to define trading-partner agreements, and to exchange XML messages in support of business operations. The goal is to allow all these activities to be performed automatically, without human intervention, over the Internet. The ebXML architecture has many similarities to SOAP/WSDL/UDDI, and some convergence is taking place with the adoption of SOAP in the ebXML transport specification. RosettaNet also announced its adoption of the ebXML transport. The ebXML messaging specification is based on SOAP with attachments but does not use WSDL. ebXML does add security, guaranteed messaging, and compliance with business process interaction specifications.

The ebXML initiative is sponsored by the United Nations Center for Trade Facilitation and Electronic Business (UN/CEFACT) and OASIS to research, develop, and promote global standards for the use of XML to facilitate the exchange of electronic business data. A major goal for ebXML is to produce standards that serve the same or similar purpose as EDI, including support for emerging industry-specific XML vocabularies. ebXML and Web services hold the promise of realizing the original goals of EDI, making it simpler and easier to exchange electronic documents over the Internet.

Electronic Data Interchange (EDI)

EDI began as early as the late 1960s. Over the years, there have been significant efforts to establish standards for EDI. Two significant standards efforts are in the INCITS (ANSI) ASC X12 committee and UN/EDIFACT (United Nations/Electronic

Data Interchange for Administration, Commerce, and Transport). These standards groups are also working with the ebXML and RosettaNet groups.

Enterprise Service Bus (ESB)

An ESB is software that makes it easier to transfer data and instructions among various software systems: services, business processes, applications, legacy systems, software agents, BI software, and so on. See page 62.

eXtensible Access Control Markup Language (XACML)

XACML provides fine-grained control of authorized activities, the effect of characteristics of the access requestor, the protocol over which the request is made, authorization based on classes of activities, and content introspection.

eXtensible rights Markup Language (XrML)

XrML is a digital rights language designed for securely specifying and managing rights and conditions associated with various resources including digital content as well as services.

eXtensible Stylesheets Language (XSL)

XSL is a language for expressing stylesheets. It consists of three parts: XSL Transformations (XSLT), a language for transforming XML documents; the XML Path Language (XPath), an expression language used by XSLT to access or refer to parts of an XML document (XPath is also used by the XLink specification); and XSL Formatting Objects (XSLFO), an XML vocabulary for specifying formatting semantics. An XSL stylesheet specifies the presentation of a class of XML documents by describing how an instance of the class is transformed into an XML document that uses the formatting vocabulary.

Extract, Transform, and Load (ETL)

ETL products are used to migrate data from one source to some destination, usually a database. The source can be a database or most any other source. The "extract" part is to select data from the source, "transform" reformats and possibly corrects the extracted data, and "load" places the transformed data into the destination database. See also Data Warehouse and data mart in this guide. See page 139.

Failover

Failover is the process of a secondary machine taking over for a primary machine. For database failover, see Replication in this guide. See page 167.

HTTP

HTTP stands for HyperText Transfer Protocol. It is a mechanism for sending requests and responses between computers connected to the Internet or an intranet.

Hybrid Cloud

A hybrid cloud is a combination of public clouds, community clouds, private clouds, and virtual private clouds. See page 42.

Infrastructure as a Service (IaaS)

Cloud providers in the IaaS category provide an infrastructure that contains the physical and virtual resources used to build the cloud. These cloud providers provision and manage the physical processing, storage, networking, and hosting environment. This is the data center or, in some cases, the data centers. Pricing is often based on resources used. See page 42.

Internet Inter-ORB Protocol (IIOP)

IIOP is the protocol used for communication between CORBA ORBs. See also CORBA in this guide.

Java API for XML Parsing (JAXP)

JAXP allows developers to easily use XML parsers in their applications.

JSON

JSON (JavaScript Object Notation) uses name/value pairs instead of the tags used by XML. See page 28.

Load Leveling

Load leveling is a design strategy that spreads activity or *load* across more than one machine. See page 168.

Loosely Coupled

Loosely coupled is a design concept where the internal workings of one service are not "known" to another service. All that needs to be known is the external behavior of the service. This way, the underlying programming of a service can be modified and, as long as external behavior has not changed, anything that uses that service continues to function as expected. See page 31.

Mapping

Mapping is the technique used to make one or more rows in database tables appear as programming language objects or XML. See www.service-architecture.com.

Mashups

A combination of data from multiple services using Web services APIs with the intent of making the data more useful or easier to visualize. See also Application Programming Interface (API) in this guide.

Message Router

Message routers direct data from a requesting resource to a responding resource and back. These are also known as application brokers or message brokers. A router "knows" which of the other internal systems needs to receive certain types of updates. The individual internal systems can pass updates to a router and would not need to know who receives such updates. A message router usually needs to transform the data in some way to match the format of the data expected by the receiving system. See page 62.

Meta-Object Facility (MOF)

The MOF is a set of standard interfaces that can be used to define and manipulate a set of interoperable meta-models and their corresponding models.

Middleware

Middleware hides the complexity of the communication between two or more systems or services. This simplifies the development of those systems and services and isolates the complexity of the communication between them. The different systems or services can be on the same hardware or on different hardware. See page 57 and 151.

Model Driven Architecture (MDA)

MDA is an open, vendor-neutral approach to interoperability using OMG's modeling specifications: Unified Modeling Language (UML), Meta-Object Facility (MOF), and Common Warehouse Metamodel (CWM).

.NET

Microsoft .NET is a set of Microsoft software technologies for Web services. Microsoft .NET is made up of three core components:

1. .NET building block services
2. .NET device software for devices such as mobile phones, pagers, and so on
3. .NET infrastructure

NoSQL Database Management System

NoSQL database management systems are generally meant to work with big data. NoSQL is usually defined as "not only SQL." They may have different locking and concurrency models compared to traditional database management systems. See also Big Data in this guide. See page 74.

Object Request Broker (ORB)

The ORB is middleware that uses the CORBA specification. See also CORBA in this guide. See page 57.

OMG Interface Definition Language (IDL)

The IDL permits interfaces to objects to be defined independent of an object's implementation. After defining an interface in IDL, the interface definition is used as input to an IDL compiler that produces output to be compiled and linked with an object implementation and its clients. See also CORBA. (There are other uses of the IDL initialism. For example, there is also a Java IDL.)

Partner Interface Process (PIP)

A PIP defines business processes between trading partners. PIPs fit into seven clusters, or groups of core business processes, that represent the backbone of the trading network. Each cluster is broken down into segments—cross-enterprise processes involving more than one type of trading partner. Within each segment are individual PIPs. PIPs are specialized system-to-system XML-based dialogs. Each PIP specification includes a business document with the vocabulary and a business process with the choreography of the message dialog.

Platform as a Service (PaaS)

Cloud providers in the PaaS category provide a complete computing platform. They provision and manage cloud infrastructure as well as provide development, deployment, and administration tools. Here you will find the features that make a platform: operating systems, web servers, programming language, database management systems, and so on. This is where the provider might provide elasticity: the ability to scale up or scale down as needed. See page 42.

Public Cloud

A public cloud allows multiple organizations to provide multiple types of services (often referred to as *multitenancy*). The location for the underlying data center could be most anywhere in the world (often referred to as *location independence*). The underlying hardware is usually chosen by the cloud provider and not the users of the service (here you will likely find *virtualization* and *device independence*). The public cloud can also be described as an *external cloud* when viewed from within a given organization. See page 41.

Registry

A registry is a network service that identifies resources on a network and makes them accessible to users and applications. For Web services, directories could use UDDI or the ebXML directory. For an example, See page 20.

REgular LAnguage Description for XML (RELAX)

RELAX is a specification for describing XML-based languages. It is standardized by INSTAC XML SWG of Japan. Under the auspices of the Japanese Standard Association (JSA), this committee develops Japanese national standards for XML. See also RELAX NG.

RELAX NG

The purpose of this committee is to create a specification for a schema language for XML based on TREX and RELAX. The key features of RELAX NG are that it does not change the information set of an XML document and supports XML namespaces, unordered content, and mixed content.

Replication

Replication is the process of making multiple copies of data on separate machines. The replicated data will be available on the secondary machine should it need to take over when the primary machine fails. See page 168.

Representational State Transfer (REST)

Representational state transfer (REST) is a style of architecture based on a set of principles that describe how networked resources are defined and addressed. REST is an alternative to the World Wide Web Consortium's (W3C) set of standards that include SOAP and other WS-* specifications. REST has proved to be a popular choice for implementing Web services. See page 22.

Resource Description Framework (RDF)

RDF is a way of describing a Web site's metadata, or the data about the data at the site.

RosettaNet Implementation Framework (RNIF)

RNIF provides the packaging, routing, and transport of RosettaNet PIP messages and business signals.

Schematron

Schematron is a language and toolkit for making assertions about patterns found in XML documents. It can be used as a friendly validation language and for automatically generating external annotation (links, RDF, perhaps topic maps). Because it uses paths rather than grammars, it can be used to assert constraints that cannot be expressed using XML schemas.

Security Assertion Markup Language (SAML)

SAML is an XML framework for exchanging authentication and authorization information.

Service

A service is a function that is well-defined, self-contained, and does not depend on the context or state of other services. See page 17.

Service-Oriented Architecture (SOA)

An SOA is essentially a collection of services. These services communicate with each other. The communication can involve either simple data passing or two or more services coordinating some activity. See page 17.

Service Provisioning Markup Language (SPML)

SPML is an XML-based framework specification for exchanging user, resource, and service-provisioning information. The SPML specification is being developed with consideration of the following provisioning-related specifications: Active Digital Profile (ADPr), eXtensible Resource Provisioning Management (XRPM), and Information Technology Markup Language (ITML).

SOAP

SOAP provides the envelope for sending Web services messages over the Internet/intranet. The envelope contains two parts:

1. An optional header providing information on authentication, encoding of data, or how a recipient of a SOAP message should process the message.
2. The body that contains the message. These messages can be defined using the WSDL specification.

SOAP commonly uses HTTP, but other protocols such as Simple Mail Transfer Protocol (SMTP) may be used. SOAP can be used to exchange complete documents or to call a remote procedure. (SOAP at one time stood for Simple Object Access Protocol. Now the letters in the acronym have no particular meaning.) See page 20.

Software as a Service (SaaS)

Cloud providers in the SaaS category provide complete software systems. SaaS is a common way to provide applications such as email, calendars, customer relationship management, social networks, content management, documentation management, and other office productivity applications. SaaS is also known as "on-demand software." See page 42.

Tree Regular Expressions for XML (TREX)

TREX is a language for validating XML documents. TREX has been merged with RELAX to create RELAX NG. All future development of TREX will take place as part of the RELAX NG effort. See also RELAX NG.

Unified Modeling Language (UML)

The UML is a specification of a graphical language used for visualizing, specifying, constructing, and documenting the artifacts of distributed object systems.

Uniform Resource Identifier (URI)

URIs, also known as URLs, are short strings that identify resources on the Web: documents, images, downloadable files, services, electronic mailboxes, and other resources.

Universal Data Model

A universal data model is a template or generic data model that can be used as a building block for the development of a data model. See page 108.

Universal Description, Discovery, and Integration (UDDI)

UDDI provides the definition of a set of services supporting the description and discovery of (1) businesses, organizations, and other Web services providers, (2) the Web services they make available, and (3) the technical interfaces that may be used to access those services. The idea is to "discover" organizations and the services that organizations offer, much like using a phone book or dialing information. See page 19.

Virtual Private Cloud

Cloud providers in this category provide some type of partitioning to ensure that the private cloud remains private. Typically, a virtual private cloud provider allows the definition of a network similar to a traditional network. Within such a network, it is possible to have systems such as database managements systems, BI/analytics systems, application servers, and so on. See page 42.

Web Distributed Data Exchange (WDDX)

WDDX is an XML-based technology that enables the exchange of complex data between Web programming languages. WDDX consists of a language-independent representation of data based on XML and a set of modules for a wide variety of languages that use WDDX.

Web Service Endpoint Definition (WSEL)

WSEL is an XML format for the description of non-operational characteristics of service endpoints, like quality-of-service, cost, or security properties.

Web Services Component Model

The Web services component model is an XML- and Web-services–centric component model for interactive Web applications. The designs must achieve two main goals: enable businesses to distribute web applications through multiple revenue channels and enable new services or applications to be created by leveraging existing applications across the Web.

Web Services Conversation Language (WSCL)

The WSCL allows the business-level conversations or public processes supported by a Web service to be defined. WSCL specifies the XML documents being exchanged and the allowed sequencing of these document exchanges. WSCL conversation definitions are themselves XML documents and can therefore be interpreted by Web services infrastructures and development tools.

Web Services Description Language (WSDL)

WSDL is a format for describing a Web services interface. It is a way to describe services and how they should be bound to specific network addresses. WSDL has three parts:

1. Definitions
2. Operations
3. Service bindings

Definitions are generally expressed in XML and include both data type definitions and message definitions that use the data type definitions. These definitions are
usually based on some agreed upon XML vocabulary. See page 19.

Web Services Experience Language (WSXL)

The WSXL enables businesses to distribute Web applications through multiple revenue
channels and to enable new services or applications to be created by leveraging existing
applications across the Web. WSXL is built on widely accepted established and emerging open standards and is designed to be independent of execution platform, browser,
and presentation markup. Interactive Web applications that are developed using WSXL
can be delivered to end users through a diversity of deployment channels: directly to a
browser, indirectly through a portal, or by embedding into a third party Web application.

Web Services Flow Language (WSFL)

The WSFL is a language for the description of Web services compositions. WSFL
considers two types of Web services compositions:

1. The appropriate usage pattern of a collection of Web services, in such a way that
   the resulting composition describes how to achieve a particular business goal;
   typically, the result is a description of a business process
2. The interaction pattern of a collection of Web services; in this case, the result is a
   description of the overall partner interactions

Web Services for Interactive Applications (WSIA)

WSIA is an XML- and Web-services–centric framework for interactive Web applications. The designs must achieve two main goals: enable businesses to distribute Web
applications through multiple revenue channels and enable new services or applications to be created by leveraging existing applications across the Web.

Web Services for Report Portals (WSRP)

WSRP is an XML and Web-services standard that will allow for the plug-and-play
of portals, other intermediary Web applications that aggregate content, and applications from disparate sources. These portals will be designed to enable businesses to

provide content or applications in a form that does not require any manual content or application-specific adaptation by consuming applications.

Web Services User Interface (WSUI)

WSUI enables Web platforms implemented in entirely different languages (Java, COM/.NET, and Perl) to interoperate and share applications. By using WSUI, an application can be packaged with a WSUI descriptor file and an XSLT stylesheet and be dynamically integrated into another website that is running a WSUI container implementation.

Workflow

Workflow refers to how two or more business processes or services might interact. See page 115.

XLANG

XLANG is a notation for the automation of business processes based on Web services for the specification of message exchange behavior among participating Web services. XLANG is expected to serve as the basis for automated protocol engines that can track the state of process instances and help enforce protocol correctness in message flows.

XML Common Biometric Format (XCBF)

XCBF is a common set of secure XML encoding for the formats specified in CBEFF, the Common Biometric Exchange File Format.

XML Encryption

XML encryption is a process for encrypting/decrypting digital content (including XML documents and portions thereof) and an XML syntax used to represent the encrypted content and information that enables an intended recipient to decrypt it.

XML Key Management Specification (XKMS)

XKMS is a specification of XML application/protocol that allows a simple client to obtain key information (values, certificates, and management or trust data) from a Web service.

XML Linking Language (XLink)

XLink allows elements to be inserted into XML documents to create and describe links between resources. It uses XML syntax to create structures that can describe the simple unidirectional hyperlinks of HTML, as well as more sophisticated links.

XML Namespaces

An XML namespaces is a collection of names, identified by a URI, which are used in XML documents as element types and attribute names. XML namespaces differ from the "namespaces" conventionally used in computing disciplines in that the XML version has internal structure and is not, mathematically speaking, a set.

XML Path Language (XPath)

XPath is the result of an effort to provide a common syntax and semantics for functionality shared between XSL Transformations and XPointer. The primary purpose of XPath is to address parts of an XML document.

XML Pointer Language (XPointer)

XPointer allows addressing the internal structures of XML documents. It allows for examination of a hierarchical document structure and choice of its internal parts based on various properties, such as element types, attribute values, character content, and relative position.

XML Protocol (XMLP)

XMLP provides simple protocols that can be ubiquitously deployed and easily programmed through scripting languages, XML tools, interactive Web development tools, etc. The goal is a layered system that will directly meet the needs of applications with simple interfaces (e.g., getStockQuote or validateCreditCard) and can be incrementally extended to provide the security, scalability, and robustness required for more complex application interfaces.

XML Schema

XML schemas express shared vocabularies and allow machines to carry out rules made by people. They provide a means for defining the structure, content, and semantics of XML documents.

XML Signature

XML Signature is an XML syntax used for representing signatures on digital content and procedures for computing and verifying such signatures. Signatures provide for data integrity and authentication.

XSL Formatting Objects (XSL-FO)

XSL-FO is a set of tools developers and web designers use to specify the vocabulary and semantics for paginated presentation.

XSL Transformations (XSLT)

XSLT is a language for transforming XML documents into other XML documents. XSLT is designed for use as part of XSL, which is a stylesheet language for XML. In addition to XSLT, XSL includes an XML vocabulary for specifying formatting. XSL specifies the styling of an XML document by using XSLT to describe how the document is transformed into another XML document that uses the formatting vocabulary. XSLT may be used independently of XSL. However, XSLT is not intended as a completely general-purpose XML transformation language. Rather it is designed primarily for the kinds of transformations that are needed when XSLT is used as part of XSL.

XQuery

XQuery is designed to be a language in which queries are concise and easily understood. It is also flexible enough to query a broad spectrum of XML information sources, including both databases and documents.

Bibliography

Further Reading

Adler, Mike. An Algebra for Data Flow Diagram Process Decomposition, *IEEE Transactions on Software Engineering*, 14(2), Feb. 1988.

Bridges, William. *Managing Transitions: Making the Most of Change*. New York: DeCapo Lifelong Books, 2009.

Fielding, Roy Thomas. Architectural Styles and the Design of Network-based Software Architectures, doctorial, available at www.ics.uci.edu/~fielding/pubs/dissertation/rest_arch_style.htm.

Humphrey, Watts S. Why Big Software Projects Fail: The 12 Key Questions. *CrossTalk: The Journal of Defense Software Engineering*, March 2005.

Humphrey, Watts S. Multi-year study of 13,000 programs conducted by the Software Engineering Institute, Carnegie Mellon. Mentioned in "Why Software Is So Bad ... and What's Being Done to Fix It," Charles C. Mann, *MSNBC Technology Review*, June 27, 2002.

Koch, Christopher. The New Science of Change, *CIO Magazine*, Oct. 2006.

Lewin, Kurt. *Field Theory in Social Science*. New York: Harper and Row, 1951.

Peter Mell and Timothy Grance. *The NIST Definition of Cloud Computing: Recommendations of the National Institute of Standards and Technology*, NIST Special Publication 800-145, September 2011, pg. 2.

Rock, David, and Jeffrey Schwartz. The Neuroscience of Leadership, *strategy + business*, Summer 2006.

Websites

Application Server Performance Gain, http://www.service-architecture.com/application-servers/articles/benchmark_using_a_transaction_accelerator.html.

Business Process Modeling Notation (BPMN), Object Management Group, http://www.bpmn.org/.

Design Decomposition for Business Process and Data Flow Diagrams, Barry & Associates, http://www.designdecomposition.com/.

Discussion of Mapping Issues, http://www.service-architecture.com/object-relational-mapping/articles/mapping_layer.html.

Holiday Shoppers Flocking Online Create Record Breaking Sales, http://www.forbes.com/sites/anthonydemarco/2011/11/27/holiday-shoppers-flocking-online-create-record-breaking-sales/.

NoSQL, http://www.nosql-database.org/.

Organizations Developing Web Service Specifications, http://www.service-architecture.com/web-services/articles/organizations.html.

Sematic Web Wikipedia, http://en.wikipedia.org/wiki/Semantic_Web.

Service-Oriented Architecture Modeling Language (SoaML), Object Management Group, http://www.omg.org/spec/SoaML/.

Web Services Architecture, http://www.w3.org/TR/ws-arch/.

Index